Soul Setting

Soul Setting

Listen to Your Soul Instead of Your Mind

Levy

TORONTO

Copyright © 2025 Chestnut Media

Published by Chestnut Media

No part of this book may be reproduced, or stored in a retrieval system, or transmitted in any form or by any means, electronic, mechanical, photocopying, recording, or otherwise, without express written permission of the publisher.

This information, including, not limited to the texts, the graphics, images and other material contained in this book are for informational purposes only. No material on this site is intended to substitute for professional medical advice, diagnosis or treatment. Always seek the advice of your physician or other qualified healthcare provider with any questions you may have regarding a medical condition or treatment, and before undertaking a new healthcare regimen, and never disregard professional medical advice or delay in seeking it, because of something that you have heard in this program.

ISBN: Paperback 978-1-0689461-0-3
ISBN: eBook 978-1-0689461-1-0

Book design by John Lotte

Manufactured in the United States of America

*To my parents (George and Ruby,
aka Dad and Mom)*

Contents

Introduction ix
1 The Little Voice 1
2 The Sixth Sense 15
3 My Journey 37
4 To Believe or Not Believe in Goal Setting 55
5 Problems 73
6 Why People Struggle 91
7 Faith and Struggle 101
8 Stress 117
9 Trauma 135
10 Luck 145
11 How to Start Your Journey 151
12 Patience, Time, and Energy 161
13 Zen 175
14 Money 183
15 Conclusion 205
Acknowledgements 207

Introduction

One of the most important realizations in life you can make is recognizing that the world starts, ends, and is lived entirely inside your mind.

To change yourself, you must first change the way you see yourself and see others. This can only be done in the soul.

Is this book for everyone? NO.

I'm not a naïve man. There are different perspectives on life that not everyone will be able to handle—not because people lack intelligence, but because they are on their own journeys and perhaps haven't recognized certain things. I truly hope that you will think about what's being discussed in this book, and if you're not ready to make *this* journey, that's okay. Down the road, when you think about what we discussed, you may be ready to examine these perspectives. In order to change, perhaps you require a new point of view that others won't discuss with you.

Quick question for you: When you eat a doughnut, will you gain thirty pounds immediately? No, of course you won't—it would take dozens of doughnuts and months (at least) to gain that kind of weight. If you save $50 per week, will you be wealthy overnight? No, of course not—it would take time to accumulate a vast sum of money.

I will show you the physical, spiritual, and financial way to change your life. This book is going to dive deep into soul setting, and if you consider my fifty-plus years on this Earth, and how I'm really winning within my own soul, you'll see that it's benefited my entire life, health, wealth, and spirituality. It can benefit yours as well.

And let me get this out there for anyone who may ask: I'm a Christian man who believes this world has a higher power. For me, my higher power is God. But relax—I'm not going to try to baptize anyone or give a sermon. My belief creates my faith for the future. Whatever you believe your higher power is, it's cool with me. I'm not trying to convert anyone. Instead, I want the book to be an enjoyable and interesting experience for everyone.

Let's get started!

I never have a negative thought come into my mind; I just have bad ideas.

/ Levy /

The Little Voice

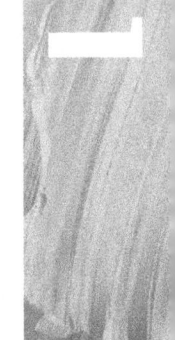

There's a "little voice" we all hear, the one that's smarter than we are but that we rarely listen to.

For example, have you ever thought about doing something in the here and now and don't do it—and then after the fact, realize YOU should have? Say you're heading home on a Friday after a long week of work. You're tired, and you're looking forward to that nice glass of wine or bottle of beer. No, not just looking forward to it—you can *taste* it. You press just a little harder on the gas.

Gas. You're low on gas. And you know that tomorrow morning, you must drive your son to hockey practice, and for some reason that defies explanation, hockey practice is always at an ungodly early hour in the morning. Once you get home, you know there won't be enough gas to get to practice.

I should stop and get gas on the way home, and then I can not only have my beer, but I won't have to stop on the way to practice tomorrow.

Action is the key to all success

/ Pablo Picasso /

You see how smart that little voice is? Should we listen to it, and do what it says? Of course we should.

But do we? No, practically never. In this case, we actively look for reasons not to. I'm too tired to stop, you think. It'll only get me home later. And that beer—that beer is practically *calling* to me. I know, you think: I'll wake up just a bit earlier and get the gas in the morning. Problem solved, right?

Not exactly. Because when you get home, that beer turns into two beers. Or maybe three. Not the entire six-pack, mind you, but enough to get a pleasant buzz going and to help you forget about the miserable week at work you just had. AND, just your luck, there's a great game of (insert your favorite game here) on TV, and it's gone into overtime or extra innings or whatever your game goes into, right? You watch the end of the game, and you fall asleep during the post-game show. Life is good.

That is, until you wake up in your chair at 3:30 in the morning. For a moment, you have no idea where you are. You sit up, and there's a crick in your neck and three empty beer cans on the table next to you. You stand and stagger to bed.

The next thing you know, your son is standing over you. "Wake up!" he says. "We're late!" And now you're rushing around trying to get ready to go, throwing yourself into clean clothes, and wondering if you have time to brush your teeth. Your son is mad at you and your spouse is yelling at you and there's still that damned crick in your neck and there's one other thing that you knew you forgot . . .

Gas.

You're not going to make it to practice without stopping to get gas. Which is only going to make your son madder and your spouse yell louder, and now that beer you drank last night just didn't taste as good as you remember it tasting. Because if you had only listened to that little voice last night, you wouldn't suddenly have problem after problem after problem mounting on your shoulders. If only you had made different choices, you'd be basking in the early morning sunlight and listening to birds chirping, rather than stumbling around your house with your pants half on and a toothbrush sticking out of your mouth, your family furious at you, and the precious moments until your son's practice begins ticking away ceaselessly.

The little voice inside you *told you* to get gas, didn't it? If you're like most people, though, instead of vowing to listen to the little voice next time, you curse that stupid little voice and wish that it would shut up and mind its own business. No little voice tells *me* what to do, you think.

The problem, however, is that the little voice *was* you—or more accurately, it was your soul. It was your soul guiding you to do the right thing. Not the right thing morally or ethically, but the right thing for your happiness and well-being. That voice was a source of higher and deeper intelligence, one that (unlike the mind) isn't driven by inadequacy or scarcity or insecurity. It's a higher intelligence that recognized what was happening in the here and now and gave up trying to control the situation. It's an intelligence that respects reality and accepts that IT JUST IS, and nothing can change that.

You can call that voice what you will: instinct, intuition, the super-ego, what have you. I prefer to think of this as your *soul*. It's your soul trying to take care of you . . . if you'll only listen.

I think one of the most important realizations in life is the recognition that the world starts, ends, and is lived *almost entirely inside one's mind.*

To change this, to change yourself, you first have to change the way you see yourself and others. This can only be done within the *soul.*

Take the poor sap running around trying to get his son to practice. His soul told him what to do, and he didn't listen. Now he's in for a miserable day full of tension, recriminations, and anger. If he lives his life largely in the same fashion, those conflicts heap and grow until they become a plague in his mind. Left unchecked, these conflicts grow both at home and at work. A lifetime of these conflicts often results in depression, anxiety, addiction, and trauma—all because he's in a state of *mind setting* and not *soul setting.*

Obviously, the example I've presented here is an exaggeration. Your life isn't going to fall apart for want of a tank of gas (at least I hope it's not). But if you're reading this book—even if you're skimming through it in the bookstore wondering whether to buy it—chances are your life is in a place where you don't want it to be. Like the guy with the empty tank of gas, your life is infested with conflict. Maybe you're dealing with depression and anxiety; maybe you're fighting addiction or maybe you're still trying to heal the scars of trauma, even trauma that goes all the way back to childhood.

I'm here to tell you that no matter what's happened to you or how bad things seem to be in your life, you're most likely there because you've grown accustomed to *mind setting,* a way of life for which the success rate is very low. When you've learned to adapt to *soul setting,* you'll learn how to give up control and accept things at a deeper, more spiritual level. You'll learn that IT JUST IS, that there are some things you can change and there are some things you just can't, and you'll be perfectly okay with that. You'll learn to listen to that little voice, and you'll learn what a powerful and effective guide it can be as you live a life of awareness of your decisions, thoughts, and emotions.

How did I come to discover all of this? Let's just say that I lived a great deal of my life in a state of mind-set rather than soul-set. So, let's take a look at the difference between the two.

Mind setting is structured to feed positive affirmations and manifestations on a daily basis. It's structured to have you live in a semi-permanent world of dreaming. As you get older, and you get far away from what you think you want to do versus what you should actually do, your life becomes a ball of stress. And sure, you continue to go down that path of insanity and continue to bolster your repeated failures with something that will ease the pain: drugs (whether they be illegal, prescribed, or recreational), alcohol, food, material possessions, isolation . . . the list goes on.

We tend to live through our twenties from a financial standpoint. What job pays a lot? How can I become rich, or even just comfortable? We look at it from a "making" standpoint versus a "creating" standpoint. Most people don't make a million dollars per year. Most people will never come close. Leave that to the star athletes, models, actors, and Fortune 500 CEOs (and yes, you may become one of those; after all, someone must).

Mind setting is the ability to manipulate your brain to prepare it for something it really isn't ready for: the constant discipline and patience you require to wait for something you're wishing for. When you're on the wrong path, what happens? Failure after failure occurs. And then, what's next? Your mind is plagued by self-doubt, a lack of confidence, fear, stress, and worry. Now you think you have problems—and really, nobody has problems, they just have situations and circumstances that they themselves created. At that point, you begin to blame your environment, the government, your parents, your upbringing, your financial situation. And now you begin to see how the mind tends to wander in different directions.

Now I invite you to look at soul setting, where you're completely aware of your conscious decision-making, and where the motives for your decision-making come from. For example, when you make a decision based on making money, are you making it from a greed standpoint, or perhaps a desperation standpoint? Are you about to be kicked out of your house or apartment? Is your car about to be repossessed? At this point, decisions are made with the mind and not the soul. You may be saying to yourself, "Well, sorry, I need to do what I need to do." But at this point, you generally wind up in a worse situation than what you were originally in. And you still get removed from your living situation, and your car is still gone. What to do then?

Easy. If you have truly exhausted all your options way in advance of these things occurring, then there isn't anything more you can do but accept the fact that this situation or circumstance is occurring. Relax, breathe, and everything will be okay. I know it really doesn't feel like it will, but it will.

Soul setting is the ability to accept everything as it is. Being okay with the way things are. Because believe me, there are a whole lot of things that you think you can control, but you can't.

Learning to be okay with life at any given moment is a superpower. This is soul setting in the extreme, and that is where I would love you to be. When it comes to decision-making, let it come from your soul, and what your soul is actually telling you. Listen to it, and let it guide you to greater things that you can't see at the moment. When anxiety and depression set in, you can be sure that it is your mind creating these states, not your soul. When soul setting is in place properly, your mind automatically follows, so there is no need to work on your mind setting. It's simply unnecessary.

This obviously takes time and practice. You will revert back to your old ways from time to time, but you will be able to catch yourself when stress occurs, and you can say to yourself, "Oh yeah, that's my mind talking to me, not my soul."

The mind/ego frequently wants things. The Rolex watch. The Gucci bag. The BMW. The nice house. That isn't your soul talking to you. It's okay; it's natural to want these things—I would love to have them as well. But when you get fixated on them, that's your mind talking to you, and the more you fixate on them, the further from soul setting you get. I know when I turned fifty, I took a hard look at my life. I was hundreds of thousands of dollars in debt and no closer to the objects that I was fixated on.

Learning to control your mind can be extremely beneficial from a health perspective. The mind/ego does not like silence. Right now, if you stop reading for a second and just sit there, I bet you can't *not* think of anything. It's impossible. So, when narratives arrive of a life that's challenging to you, your ego goes into overdrive and starts imagining negative outcomes.

If you're soul setting, however, you can (in time)

immediately recover from this state and realize, "it's okay, it's just my mind talking to me." Too many people can't do this—they're slave to their thoughts. "What if he/she doesn't like me?" "What if I don't get this promotion?" "What if I can't pay my bills this month?" The list goes on and on. But this type of thought pattern can be eradicated when you live in your *soul* and not your *mind*. Breathing and understanding that life is going to happen whether you worry about it or not will help you realize that worrying isn't going to change the outcome of the challenges you face in life.

Let's look at an outcome that isn't desirable. Let's say you're up for a promotion. You're excited to get it, and your mind is telling you, "You *must* get it. Imagine what you can do with this increase in financial status. Imagine the things you can buy." Immediately, you're creating a circumstance that isn't healthy. You're speaking from the ego and not the soul.

And now the news comes in that you didn't get the promotion. What happens to you? Extreme disappointment. Possibly depression. Of course, it's only human to be disappointed, but remember: this was something over which you had very little control (sort of like the rest of your life, yes?). Your mind goes into overdrive, and you start asking yourself things like, "What did I do wrong?" and "I'm more qualified than the person who got the job!" When in fact, you didn't do anything wrong; IT JUST IS! Period. Analyzing it to death will not change anything but your health and well-being.

Now let's look at it from the soul perspective. Let's look at the same promotion. My ego is neutral; whether I get this promotion or not is just fine with me. That's right—when practicing soul setting, your outlook on life is to have no preference in these kinds of situations. I'm still trying to master this because, after all, I'm human, and there are certain situations in which I would prefer certain outcomes. I don't go into job interviews with an "I don't care" attitude. I still give it my all and act as if I already have the job.

What I do, however, is make sure my ego is okay with the decision that's about to occur, one over which I have zero control. Doing the best I can is all I can do.

So now the decision has been made, and I didn't get the promotion. How do I feel? With soul setting, I'm completely neutral. I'm okay with the situation and the circumstances. I understand what has happened JUST IS. I have faith in life and that God (or your higher power) is always looking out for me. Maybe the boss I was going to get was going to be difficult to work with. Maybe that job was going to be phased out in three months, making me unemployed. Maybe in another month, a better promotion will come up. Any number of scenarios could play out.

How do I know if I'm practicing soul setting correctly, and I'm still not simply mind setting? This is easy to figure out. If you didn't get that promotion, you become upset, possibly depressed. We know this is the mind and the ego doing this. If soul setting is in place, you're okay with the situation. You're fine deep in your soul. You have to be—what other choice do you have?

As you practice soul setting, you see that your stress level decreases dramatically. Your overall outlook on life improves because you understand that God has more in store for you than you think. This must be practiced endlessly. "My best days are ahead of me" is just as probable as, "I will never have any chance and my life is over." And choosing the former over the later will do wonders for your well-being, as well.

Soul setting is the ability to stop thinking with your mind and start thinking with your soul. It's understanding that life happens. IT JUST IS. It's having faith that the future will look after you. The future will happen whether you do something or not. When you adopt this lifestyle, your energy changes, and you start to have inner peace. You will accept life as it happens, and you'll be okay with it, because you have to be. If you don't like life as it's happening, look at what you can control, which is usually your inner self. As you enter self-awareness (or spiritual awareness), you will enter a freedom that you've never felt before.

Let me tell you something about myself: I used to drink. A lot. I was an alcoholic. The reason I drank so much is that it was a coping mechanism. It was how I dealt with stress. Now that the stress is gone, I have no use for alcohol, because I don't have to COPE with life anymore. I just live it.

From the depths of my soul, I can tell you that the best thing I ever did was to quit drinking. And the funny thing is that the worst days of my life turned out to be the best part of my life. It was an opportunity for me to change directions. I know for a fact that my higher power was calling me and looking out for me, even though I couldn't see it at the time.

This book might be difficult for people who believe in mind setting and find that it works for them. My suggestion is twofold:

1. **Put down this book and don't go any further.** I'm not trying to convince anyone what I'm saying here is gospel. I'm one man going through life, just as you are. I've had big ambitions. I still do. This book is an accumulation of

fifty-plus years of failure after failure with very few wins. After adopting soul setting at age fifty, however, my life has had more wins than failures. My future looks bright . . .

Or . . .

2. **Go on reading the book.** This next chapter may open your eyes to a new perspective. If you're like me and you're working hard on old concepts and ideas that don't seem to work, and you are plagued by depression and anxiety and you're worried and stressed, I suggest you open your mind and give yourself a chance to grow spiritually.

IT JUST IS!

/ Levy /

The Sixth Sense

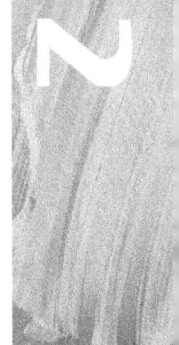

As parents, we do our children a disservice when we say, "Whatever you put your mind to, you can achieve." This is just a pure delusion. We are put here on this world for a reason, and it's not wish fulfillment. I'm sorry to burst your bubble with this news. Some of you may say it's negative thinking, but it's not. It's reality.

Do We Only Have Five Senses? (Or, The Sixth Sense)

We're all familiar with the five senses: sight, smell, hearing, taste, and touch. These are the more well-known senses that we use. These senses are generally what allow us to live as human beings.

Whatever the mind can conceive and believe, it can achieve.

/ Napoleon Hill /

But we do have another sense that, for the most part, many of us don't realize we have. It's not your fault; we just don't talk about it. This is where soul setting comes into play.

I like to call this the sixth sense (and no, contrary to the movie of the same name, it has nothing to do with seeing dead people). If you practice using this sense and pay attention to it internally, I believe it can make a huge difference in your life. This sense is in every one of us. As you pay attention to this sense, it does, in time, become part of you and your identity. As a matter of fact, this sense is responsible for my transformation in all aspects of my life.

Soul setting can be called many things: intuition, unconscious knowledge, cognition, inner sense, insight, or unconscious pattern recognition. It begins in your soul, a place where your individual life-force resides. We're all born with one. To be attuned to your soul is to further your life on this planet in a capacity that very few people are aware of. It enhances your being. The soul is an energy that never escapes any of us. The energy that revolves around the world (in my belief, God), can be a magnet once you understand and harmonize with your soul on this level.

Benefits of Soul Setting

Inner peace
Reduction in stress
Improvement in health
Contentment

Increased faith in the future
More fulfilling relationships
Gratitude
Increased wealth

INNER PEACE

I'm not sure why anyone wouldn't want this in his or her life. I believe it's because people think it's three hours of voodoo, meditation, burning incense, and cultivating a monk-life life. This couldn't be further from the truth. If you're reading this book, chances are you're looking for change—and not just small changes, but major changes in your life. All human functions stem from the soul. Everything, from the spiritual to the psychological to the physiological—this basically is LIFE.

Can you imagine what you could do with your life if you were free of distraction? Someone could cut you off in traffic, and it's okay. Someone could bad-mouth you; it's okay. You could have minor setbacks; it's fine. This new life would create new energy for you. This new energy would allow for new and often better opportunities to come into your life—opportunities that weren't allowed to come in before because your negative energy was always there in front of you. You would no longer be in distress, fighting against the outside world. Whatever happens, happens.

A perfect life to me is a life in which I have no preferences. For example, if I'm looking for an apartment and two of them present themselves, I try not to have a preference. And this is still true even if I get both of them. But wait—I need an apartment. Of course I do. The very fact that I don't have a preference whether I get one or not sends an energy out into the world (and in my belief system, God) that I believe things will work out the way IT JUST IS; not the way it is supposed to, but just is. Period.

REDUCTION IN STRESS

Can you imagine a world where you just accept the outside world with all of its flaws according to your inside world? These aren't flaws at all. The outside world is doing what it is supposed to do. It may not work the way you want it to; you may think the world is moving to slow for what you want, but regardless of what you think the world will always work out in your best interest even if you don't see it at the time. Being realistic with life, and not delusional, will assist you in your stress-free life.

Do I get everything I want in life? According to the outside world I do, but sometimes I must admit my inside world gets a little tested from time to time. I have issues that creep up. For example, my wife and I are in real estate. When a property is presented to us, sometimes, although those times are decreasing, I have a preference in wanting it. I have to shake my head and remember soul setting. There is a saying by Ave Mateiu that I am sure you have heard: "Little by little, day by day, what is meant for you WILL find its way," and another by r.m. drake, "Everything that is meant for you will find you. From people. To moments. To things. If it is for you, it will come. And when it does, be there. Enjoy, live and love."

My whole life creed is based upon this premise. Faith that

things ALWAYS work out for my best interest, even when I don't understand. It's not up to me to understand or put each puzzle piece together because I can't see one hundred percent of the parts that are coming my way. Your purpose, remember, is to spiritually grow and to help others. That's it.

I hear it all the time, and as you are reading this you are saying, but what if it doesn't happen the way it is supposed to? It will not happen the way it is supposed to be, IT JUST IS and that means your soul setting isn't in place properly you are still in mind setting. Being self-aware of this is awesome, not bad. It means you still have places to grow. As a matter of fact, until the good Lord calls me home, I will still have more work to do, but I understand it won't be finished.

HEALTH IMPROVEMENTS

Stress creates more physical ailments than any other one component. When you look at certain cancers, heart issues, sleep issues, and a whole host of immune system deficiencies, stress alone is a major factor in these health issues. When you are seventy, eighty, ninety plus years old, do you not want a quality of life in which you are not bedridden, oxygen dependent, or dependent on some form of a walking aid? Here is your chance to perhaps change the future. Of course, I cannot predict or guarantee that you won't get cancer or have other health issues, but to understand and look around at the number of people in their sixties plus with major health concerns that perhaps, and I really believe this, would feel differently if only they were stress free. People always say to me that you can't live a stress-free life. I am not saying one hundred percent stress free, but maybe ninety percent stress free, because that is how much control you have. Ninety percent of the issues, circumstances, or situations that occur in your life are drama issues you can do without.

It is a proven fact medically that your psychological issues or situations are directly related to your physiological problems. Meaning you can cure ailments with the direction of your soul.

Addictions come to mind when we band-aid psychological issues. It's a vicious cycle, that will affect you from a physical stand point. Find a solution for your psychological issue beyond soothing with addictions, and your health will improve dramatically. Soul setting is that solution.

Some examples of physiological issues:

> Depression
> Anger
> Lack of sleep
> Gastro-Abdominal issues
> Trembling
> Seizures

Some examples of psychological issues:

> Not capable of stopping drug usage.
> Abusing drugs even when health problems arise.
> Using narcotics to deal with life's problems.
> Obsession.
> Taking a gamble.
> Taking larger doses.

When gathered, you can have social issues:

Forfeiting activities.

Discarding hobbies.

Solitude.

Denial.

Excessive consumption.

Having stashes.

Legal issues.

Financial difficulties.

The world seems to be getting to be a more difficult place to live, but it isn't as long as you don't conform and compare yourself to others. Your definition of success plays a large part in this scenario we call life. With the technological advancements in the world, and your life on video and in pictures (YouTube, Tik Tok, Instagram, Facebook, etc.) it amazes me how many people are fake. Life isn't all about going to the Cayman Islands for six months of the year at the age of twenty-seven, rolling in money. Now don't get me wrong there are twenty-seven-year-olds doing this, but from a realistic standpoint your odds are incredibly low. Is this a lifestyle that people this age are going to sustain for the rest of their life? I doubt it because as they play, life will pass them by.

Far too many people are suffering in this world, and they don't need to be. I really believe it is the utter disconnect they have with the sixth sense. They live in a world that only can conceive of the five senses that are within the physical realm. It's not your fault. How can you know about a topic that can change your life if nobody brings this knowledge to you?

When you compare yourself to others, it's based on what you can see or hear only. You see them driving their Porsche, or you hear how much money they "presume" to have based on their possessions or their occupation.

For example, everyone thinks that doctors and lawyers make a ton of money. In a perfect world, if you look at the average household income, yes, they probably do make more. With this occupation, do you think they need to embody the image of that occupation? Society has dictated and drowned people's minds with an image. An image many doctors and lawyers can't keep up with. What if I told you there are large portions of them who live paycheck to paycheck just like you do. The only difference is you don't see it. All you see are materialistic things they own. Well, how do you think they pay for them? The salary they bring in? Tell me what the difference is of someone making $40,000 and spending $2,000 a month on toys, versus someone making $100,000 spending $5,000 on toys. Nothing. They are spending the exact same from a percentage basis.

Let's look at your life. When you get a raise, what happens with that extra money. Chances are you spend it, or you increase your lifestyle just to keep up with the Joneses. We all have purposes in life, and one of those purposes is to help others. In doing that, we should really increase our donations. This is one of the building steps to wealth building. Not very many people talk about it.

PLEASE DON'T CONFORM WITH WHAT YOU SEE AND THINK THE WORLD SHOULD LOOK LIKE, BASED ON OUTSIDE STIMULUS.

CONTENTMENT

Are you sick and tired of people saying, "I just want a happy life and to be happy"? That is their life goal. If you could do that, that'd be awesome. I understand what people want. It's the same thing everyone wants, just a life that isn't full of drama and stress; they want that inner peace, they want to stop that chattering in the mind. Here is the issue! You can't have a HAPPY life and be happy. It's impossible. Happiness is an emotion not a state. I think what you should be striving for is a content life, a content life with many happy moments in it. Contentment is so overrated. Relax, my definition of contentment ISN'T to resonate to a life of "ho hum, I am here" attitude. I didn't say just to accept life as it comes by doing nothing. When people hear Levy say, "Strive for a content life," they get this message mixed up. It's not that you will get the life you want sitting on the couch eating potato chips and having a beer and the door will knock and someone will say, "Hey, are you looking for a $100,000 salary career?" Life doesn't happen that way. You do need to put a huge effort into life if you expect huge things back. My definition of a "Content Life" is to accept the outside world as it is. You can't control the outside world, you can't control if someone else buys your dream house, gets the dream promotion you were interviewed for, or even if your car is repossessed because the company you worked for after fifteen years went bankrupt.

STORY TIME

I lived for eighty-five percent of my life striving for happiness, and my happiness was money and success. My definition of success was a great title at work with lots of money behind it. If only I knew what I know now. At fifty, I revaluated my life. My life was bad at that age. I had given up. Not the traditional giving up, but I stopped chasing money among other things. I accepted I could be in a content state about the results happening around me with happy moments in them. Today, I own a real estate building company. We build investment opportunities for ourselves. I have schedules I should adhere to for foundation, framing, electrical, plumbing HVAC, etc. . . . but I don't. I can't stand schedules. In this business I have so many people I know who are stressed out because they are always behind in their schedules. I should be stressed as well because issues always arise in this business, but I'm not, at least I try not to be. I work hard, plan and do the best I can to get these buildings built as fast as I can, but if it takes me two months longer than the average builder, that is A-OK with me. The guys who work for me do not need me to pass down the stress to them, and that is what I see with other companies. I hear it all the time. I am content with the process of each build as it happens. They will get done when they are supposed to get done.

INCREASED FAITH IN THE FUTURE

As I mentioned, I am a Christian, so my higher power is God. Now this book is not trying to convert anyone; however, whatever your higher power is, I really lean into my higher power. With soul setting, if you understand and practice it daily, and yes hourly when it comes to decisions on how to react to situations and individuals, you increase your faith that a bright future is always ahead of you. Your present may not seem to be very bright, but accept what is going on around you, that your higher power always has your back. It may not seem like it sometimes. Let's take a look at an example of your own life. You may be going through something right now, and if you aren't that is awesome, but try to think of a time in your life that was difficult. For some of you, you may be constantly bringing it forward in your life today. If you are, that is struggling, and you are resisting it. If you got through your tough time, you remember at the time it was not fun. When looking at that situation now, you can see perhaps how things have gotten together for you, or aligned for you, for the better.

My faith has increased daily, and I mean daily. People irritate me from time to time, but I just empathize for them with compassion. They don't know any better for the most part. Faith now lives so deep in my soul that I really understand that my higher power is ALWAYS looking after my back.

MORE FULFILLED RELATIONSHIPS

I have to admit I do not have a lot of relationships. This is by design. I expect a lot from myself, so I expect a lot from others. It's not that I am better than anyone, but this life is very short and I want to make the best of it and with whom I want to have a relationship with. I see no need for unnecessary drama or stress in my life. If I wanted negative energy in my life, I can do that myself, thank you very much. I choose to stay away from people who complain, do not take responsibility for their own actions, negative people, and the list could go on.

Do you know what the sad part about this is. There are family members I have that do not contribute anything to my life. This used to bother me to no end. I was the one to call or make lunch dates or communicate with them. Never did it reciprocate. This took me years to get through and I realized it was my issue not theirs. I took full responsibility and decided to consciously choose to distance myself from them. Sure, I see them from time to time and I act as if nothing is wrong. because you know something, I don't think they really care because nothing is said in passing like, "Hey, we should get together for lunch." Over the short years that I have lived with this, my stress level has dropped. I have a saying I teach my adult children that if I am not going to be a priority in your life, then you won't be a priority in mine. "But Levy, they are family." I understand but explain to me why you should be a door mat and be treated poorly. Would you except this from so-called friends? I doubt it.

My door is always open to my relatives to create a new relationship based on respect, and I continually pray that things will change. Until then, I keep my distance.

Now for other relationships that have deepened. The relationships I am talking about are relationships with strangers, people who perhaps you can only tolerate in small doses, and fake friends. When you get into soul setting you understand people and their behaviors. Remember, it is based on their past history, experiences and the people who raised them with the values and morals they have, so really, it's not their fault up until now. They don't know any better for the most part. I treat these people with compassion and empathy. I don't usually get mad at people because I don't have to. It doesn't mean I don't agree with their opinion, but I don't show it.

The energy I have is so positive that I can really pour into the very few relationships I have and give one hundred percent into them, and this includes my wife. I don't need to come home from work and dump on her. Doesn't it make sense to get rid of negative friends, limit your interaction with negative family members, because let's face it, I JUST DON'T NEED IT, AND NEITHER DO YOU.

GRATITUDE

Every evening (and we don't miss many), my wife and I lie together in bed and we ask, "What are you grateful for today?" We don't have to list ten things, just one simple thing that made your day go great. There is always something. I will have to admit that lying there, I sometimes struggle to come up with something. This is brutal because there are so many things, like breathing, eating, didn't have an accident, nobody in your family had an accident, but these are common appreciations we take for granted. We really try hard to come up with something out of the unusual. How do I do this? Self-Awareness. Each day as we go through it there is usually something unique that happens that you are grateful for. For example, you could be driving and it's slippery out. You go into a slide and you control it like Mario Andretti and regain control of the car as another car approaches. Whew, an accident averted. Tell me that isn't something to be grateful for, but we go on with our day and say nothing to no one, especially your higher power. Another simple example for me happened the other day. I went to the hardware store for a tube of silicone to finish the house we were working on to sell. The type of silicone I wanted was sold out. I went to four other places and nothing. I decided to go home and see if I had any other tubes at home, thinking, "I don't, but I better check." Voila! A brand-new tube was just sitting there waiting for me. I really didn't think I had that kind of thing at home. Simple eh, I sure was grateful. I say to myself, "Well it looks like I have my blessing for my wife when she asks."

As you go through your life, be self-aware of what is going on. When you practice this, you will be really surprised at how many blessings come your way on a daily basis. My wife and I get so good that often, more than one blessing comes up.

By verbalizing these random acts each day, your energy is rewarded with a renewed spirit or zest for life. The negative isn't allowed into your soul because you're grateful.

INCREASED WEALTH

You notice that this is in last place. I know you hear this often, but I really don't believe it to be true. Money isn't that important, or there is more to life than money. Here is my truth. Money is important because without it, how do you pay your bills, how do you eat and pay for shelter? It's just that simple. I just want to live comfortably. What does that mean? People say this all the time to me. They usually reply, I just want to be able to pay the bills, eat, pay for my rent, maybe go on a nice trip once a year. They never mention investing money or donating money. Sure, they say they would like a little nest egg, but that is where it lies.

When you understand soul setting and what it can do for you, the opportunities that it delivers because of the negative energy you no longer transmit, it's quite exciting. You don't have problems anymore because you understand that this is life, and those problems are merely situations and circumstances you need to deal with. That's it. People don't bother you like they used to because you understand their history, experiences, the way they were raised, values, beliefs, and morals. Everyone is different. How you value money is important, but you no longer have to chase it, it will chase you. The career you choose is the career you love and it's not just a nine to five job. No, you don't have to be self-employed or an entrepreneur to enjoy life and the abundance of money it offers. The material objects that you used to just go out and purchase to keep up with the Joneses you no longer covet as frequently as you once did. You no longer compare yourself to this world. You are doing your own thing. Understanding it's not how much money you make, but what you do with your money. Patience and time are on your side, and you understand about wealth building through asset-producing income versus liabilities that drain your pocket. It's a different life when you think with your soul and not your mind.

The Mind-Setting Myth

WARNING! This next chapter might be difficult for some. This chapter isn't meant to be a negative chapter about mind setting. However, in my view, and after more than fifty years of working on some sort of mind setting, I've come up with this conclusion, if mind setting is working for you, then skip this chapter. Reading it though, might open up some new perspectives on mind setting you may have never considered, and it may take you to a higher level.

Let's talk about the mind and mind setting. You may have heard of such terms as:

Positive mindset

Growth mindset

Money mindset

Rich mindset

Poor mindset

Millionaire mindset

Goal-setting mindset

Fixed mindset

Abundance mindset

Fear mindset

I could list many more mindsets that you're supposed to work on. But how would you do that? Talk about information overload in your mind! It really is no wonder that when I look back at my life, all of which I spent trying to become successful, I didn't. I worked on my mind, and eventually, after fifty years, I found out that paralysis by analysis really does exist.

Your brain can get stuck in a ditch. It can be lazy and want the easy way out, so it creates patterns of familiarity and complacency. The brain doesn't thrive on change—your soul does. The soul begs to grow. When you resist change, you'll be in a constant struggle. Let life happen as it's going to happen, because let's face it, that's the way it's going to happen anyway. Your mind/ego is wired to predict situations based on past experiences and how they have worked out in the past; that's why it's so dangerous to live through your mind. It's based on your conditioning as a young person. It's the old fight or flight mode. This is where anxiety is created. Your mind is programmed from your past experiences, and when a situation arises, it will automatically try to predict the outcome. But that future isn't here yet, and neither is the outcome, so we become anxious. When you continue to bring the past forward, you're going to manifest situations that reflect that past until you recognize it. Many people don't. And that's one tough life to live.

How many times have you heard people talking about "How to control your mind and win"? There has to be a reason why most people never reach their true potential. That's what I've been trying to figure out for myself. I've spent more money than I care to admit on seminars that talk about mind setting, I've read books, I've taken more courses, seen more videos, and at the age of fifty, I was hundreds of thousands of dollars in debt and nowhere close to my potential.

Something was severely wrong with what I was doing. I gave up, so to speak, and thought, "This is as good as it will get." I continued to work hard just for the sake of employment, and I stopped chasing the almighty dollar. I tripled-down on self-awareness, the people around me, my environment, and most of all, my emotions. I couldn't stand my anger, so I worked on that and studied emotional intelligence. I was sick of struggling. I wanted peace in my life.

During this time, it didn't really take much to figure out a few things. My mind/ego was the issue. Being programmed for so many years to work on my mind was the issue. And just where should I begin to work on my mind, anyway? So many gurus were telling me about the different types of mind setting to work on. Where should I start? I was drowning in information overload.

Stop Caring

I can almost hear you as you read this. "What? Stop caring? You can't be serious?" Yes, I am, but it's not the "stop caring" you might think I mean. Of course, you should always care for yourself and others.

I had always been searching for that gold ring. I had always wanted to be wealthy, to be able to provide for myself and my family, and to help others. But it was at this point in my life that I made the decision to stop caring about money and the future. I had come to this point a few times before in my life, but this time I really meant it. I meant it *deep in my soul*. I didn't just say it with my mind, my ego. This time I had had enough.

Giving up, so to speak, and not caring was the best advice I had ever given myself. Relax—I wasn't ready to check out of this world. I was just exhausted from working so hard on my mind. This is where I came to my "ah-ha!" moment, or my epiphany, if you will. Your mind/ego is wired to predict situations; that's why it's so dangerous to live through your mind. It's based on its conditioning from when we were young people. It's the old fight-or-flight mode.

> **New mind, no mind! Make a choice!**

/ Levy /

My Journey

As I write this, I'm in my fifties—closer to sixty than fifty. At the age of fifty, my future looked bleak.

It started at the age of twenty-seven, when a failed marriage rocked my world for the next ten years, during which I was miserable, going nowhere, and drowning in self-pity. It didn't help that my ex was taking me to court every other month, it seemed, for more child support and less access time for me to spend with the kids. After throwing out good money after bad after good for lawyers, I lost everything and went bankrupt. With no money, I decided to go to my local university campus and check out the law library. From there, I started defending myself, and I didn't do too badly.

The lesson I learned from all of this is simple and powerful. What I learned is this: Everything we go through, both good and bad, is exactly what happened. That's it. (IT JUST IS, remember?) And when I suffer from depression over something that's happened to me (or from anxiety over

---

Of course I am out of my mind. It's dark and scary in there.

/ unknown /

something that I'm worried may or may not happen to me), I consider it a gift.

The gift is the state of knowing that something is off course, usually in the way that I'm thinking. I think I have a problem when I don't. The thinking I have a problem *is* the problem. Whatever the issue may be, I'm thinking about it in my mind rather than accepting it in my soul, which creates the actual conscious thoughts that I really don't want to have.

From the Beginning . . .

I was raised in a middle-class family. I have great parents, and as I write this book, they are blessed and still with us at eighty-eight- and eighty-seven-years young. They still live in the house where I was raised, and they've been there for close to sixty-five years. It isn't a huge house, but in the sixties and seventies, it was a thriving family neighborhood.

I grew up in Canada, and there wasn't much crime in our city. My childhood was wonderful. Both my parents were disciplinarians, and I knew they both loved me. They were two of the few parents that went to your baseball, volleyball, and basketball games. I come from a family of five children, and I'm a twin to a wonderful sister.

My teen years were awesome, and well into my early twenties, I had found a great career, a woman whom I thought was the love of my life, had gotten married, and had two children by the time I was twenty-six. The career was life insurance, and I was on the fast track in management with a national company. I was making $60,000 a year in the early nineties, which, with inflation taken into account, would have been more than $100,000 in 2020.

Then, everything fell apart.

When I was twenty-seven, my wife at the time lost her father to a massive heart attack right in front of the family at their cottage. She and I went on a trial separation—not my choice, but hers. Was I a perfect husband? Who is? I had developed a drinking problem. I wasn't an abusive drunk; rather, I was one of those sentimental drunks who loved to hug everyone in sight. I only drank on Fridays and Saturdays, and at special occasions like parties or weddings, but I usually overindulged.

From time to time, my wife and I argued about my drinking, but she never threatened to leave me. Our marriage wasn't perfect, but in my mind, it was good. Solid.

When my father-in-law died, my wife announced to the world that we were divorcing. I was stunned. I didn't see it coming. I thought our separation was only going to be for a couple of weeks. I thought she just needed time to think and figure things out. Our children were one and three and were the apples of my eye. When I saw that I was going to lose them, I did everything I could to win my wife back.

Immediately after the funeral though, (and I mean *immediately*) she applied for divorce and served me the papers. Again, I told myself that things would be all right, because she's still in shock.

The whole family moved into my mother-in-law's house to help support her and the debt that her husband had incurred. He had been a chiropractor, but he also owned a marina and was a silent partner in a car dealership. Money was flowing in, but he had passed away without life insurance to support the millions he had in debt. Eventually, they lost everything, and his estate went into bankruptcy.

My mother-in-law and my wife moved in together with our children. We wound up selling our house as well, and my wife took most of its contents. This was my choice. I still told myself that our separation was only temporary. I was too embarrassed to tell anyone that my marriage had ended, so I kept it a secret for the first few months. I drank every night and cried myself to sleep.

I still couldn't figure out what went wrong. Back then, divorces weren't granted without some kind of government intervention, usually counseling. I remember my first meeting like it was yesterday. It lasted for ten minutes. The counselor said that I had zero chance of rectifying the marriage. When I asked why not, he gave me the usual "patient confidentiality" lecture. So, I left with little to no idea of what was going on, suspecting only that it was my drinking. I cried all the way home. Everyone else seemed to know why she was leaving except me: the judge, her family, her lawyer—everyone.

When she moved in with another woman, I figured it out. She was a lesbian. Shocked and dismayed, I spiraled down from there. I gave up on life and started a ten-year drinking binge. I lost the job that I had for nine years, went bankrupt, and didn't care. For two years, I never dated, hoping for a miracle. Maybe she would change her mind and realize that this new life she had found wasn't for her? Of course, that never happened, and our relationship became more bitter. We fought over money and access to the kids, who I saw on Wednesday nights and every other weekend. After two years, she decided to move two and a half hours away to Toronto—a place we both had once said we didn't want to move to.

It might sound as if I'm bitter about all of this. I promise you I'm not. What has happened has already happened, and there isn't anything I can do about it. As a matter of fact, it just worked out the way. How do I know this? Because it did. The lifestyle guru Peter Crone has a quote that I try to live by, "What happened, happened, and couldn't have happened any other way . . . because it didn't." If you can get this saying deep in your soul, not just into your mind and ego, your life will be so much more beneficial in that you will *stop struggling*. The unfortunate part for me is that I never heard this quote until relatively recently.

Instead of giving up the struggle, I became a full-fledged alcoholic, drinking every day. I just didn't care. I lived in subsidized housing for a while, and while there, I met this young chap named Joshua. My son Bret brought him home one day and asked if he could stay for supper. Of course I said, as long as it was all right with his parent (he was from a broken home, too). My son was five or six years old at the time, and Josh was seven or eight. Although there was a two-year gap in between them, Josh was just as big as my boy. They became good friends, and I became accustomed to having Josh around. He stayed over on weekends and school breaks. Even when I moved, we stayed in contact with him.

Josh had a sister named Ashley, and their mother's name was Sharon. I wasn't attracted to their mother, but I remember talking to her about the choices she was making in the men she was dating.

Let's fast forward twenty years. As I got to know Sharon,

I gradually realized that I was falling in love with her, and after fifteen years, we decided to marry. Josh and Ashley became my son and daughter, and I was thrilled. Sharon and the kids have gone through my drinking days and my hard times and have always been there for me.

Why am I telling you this story?

Life has a strange way of consistently showing you where you need to grow. The struggles I went through were due to a total lack of emotional intelligence. I was one hundred percent responsible for my struggles, ninety-five percent of which were a result of my resisting them and wanting a different outcome—an outcome that I couldn't control.

It's the same with most of us. We encounter issues with relationships that we can't control (even though we think we can), and they never work out.

Jail and Suicide Planning

There I was, still suffering from depression and anxiety and on no meds, and I seemed to be getting worse. Finally, one day my drinking caught up with me, and I found myself spending the night in jail. This was quite unusual for my family—we generally weren't people who wound up in jail. My father had a very influential job for our city and county, and my mother volunteered in the community, strengthening our family name ever more. My brother was a fire inspector for the city, I had two sisters who were nurses, and a twin sister who excelled in the quality control department. We weren't a family who usually found ourselves in jail. TO make matters worse, when I got arrested, my name appeared in the local paper under Police News of the Week. I was mortified, and it just took the scandal to another level.

I remember crying while I was sitting in the cell. I remember a police officer walked by and asked me if I was okay. I never answered. I got out the next day, and my family asked me to come over to the house, and yes, I walked right into an intervention.

What did I do after my family's intervention? You guessed it—I headed right to a bar for a drink. Afterwards, on my own in my little apartment, I sat there, crying again, and contemplated taking my own life. I planned how I was going to do it. Sure, I had thought about it before, but this time was more serious.

Thankfully, I didn't go through with it. Sobbing uncontrollably, I called my dad and told him, "I need help." The next day, he took me to my doctor for an emergency visit. My sister the nurse then got involved—she hooked me up with a rehab in a nearby city. I went immediately. It was a scary place: I was on my own, away from my hometown, and I just cried as I walked the street before bed in this unfamiliar place. I can't recall how long I was there, but it wasn't more than a couple of days. This was just a temporary place to get clean.

Meanwhile I waited to get into a thirty-day rehab. I didn't drink at all, and I made it a month before I finally got into the place. For the first two weeks, I didn't talk to anyone. I was upset that I had put myself in this position. During the second half of my stay, however, I was more relaxed, and I gave into the idea of not drinking ever again.

The rehab facility turned me over to a doctor/counselor who had no idea what I was going through. During our first session, I asked him, "How long have you been clean?"

"Oh, I've never had an addiction problem," he said.

Right then and there, I asked for someone new, someone who was an addict, someone who would know from experience what I was going through. After all, how can someone teach me how to become clean if they've never been where I was at? It's like a poor person teaching you how to become a millionaire. Experience is the best teacher, after all.

The month went by, and I started my new journey. I was determined to stay clean, and I did. I've been clean ever since I left that place, and as I write this book close to eighteen years later, I've been clean ever since.

Flash forward to the age of fifty: My new wife and I had been working hard to purchase a property that had actually fallen in my lap (well, it didn't actually fall—I had been working very hard purchasing properties for so many years before that from time to time, things would randomly work out in my favor, and this was one of those things). The property was hidden in the middle of the city. It was an old church, but it didn't look like a church. It looked like a house. It had close to 4,500 square feet, with eight-foot ceilings in the basement. One issue (which to this day hasn't been an issue) was that there was a group home we had to share the property with as well as a cemetery in the backyard, but again, no problem.

We spent a year and a half with three different engineers because the city needed the property to change zoning. For some reason, the property was registered as a parkland. The parcel beside us was owned by the conservation area, so another assessment was necessary. All of this took a lot of time and more than three thousand dollars that we never had.

At this point, we still didn't own it, and I was sick and tired of it. I told my wife that I was thinking of giving up, because it was just too much. The city was killing us with everything they wanted from us. My wife, being supportive, told me, "You do what you feel is right." In the back of my mind, I told myself, "Well, if I want to build real estate, then I might as well get used to this process, because this is exactly what I'll be going through!"

I continued and I didn't quit. We spent a year and a half on this property just to reach the end. That was when the elders of the church approached me and said that we had to put a deadline on the project and at least get it on the market. I understood—after all, they had given us a year and a half. The lead elder told me that they were going to put the property on the market—*tomorrow*.

"WHAT?!" I said. I couldn't believe my ears. No warning or even, "You have until such-and-such a date, or we'll put it on the market." We were done.

I remember there were five of them. There had been only four members of this church, but for some reason, this younger guy came out of the woodwork and just started talking as if he had been there the whole time. We were fortunate that one of the elderly gentlemen had taken a shine to me, and we connected and often talked privately about what the others were saying behind our backs. Nothing bad had happened until this new guy came into the picture. I'm not sure what his motive was, but I suspected he wanted the property.

I remember piping up at the meeting and saying, "This isn't very Christian-like. I don't feel you're treating me fairly, although you have been all through the process. Why?" Their answer was because it was all taking too long. I agreed with them, but I said, to be fair, you should give me a couple of more weeks, and then we'll walk away, no questions asked.

There was some discussion, and they finally agreed. So, there we were, with two weeks left, and still, by the way, zero financing for the place. No banks, or anyone else, would touch it because it was classified as a church. I had spoken to so many people during the previous year and a half, getting just close enough for them to say "no."

The two weeks went by quickly, and we were on the last twenty-four hours. We had sold our place, and we had nowhere else to go. During that previous week, we looked for a place to live in case the church didn't work out (and it looked like it wasn't going to). We were talking to dozens of private people for the money (not a lot at the time—only $110,000). Finally, someone stepped up and said that maybe they would loan us the money. We had twenty-four hours left, and miraculously, we had found a place to live in case the church didn't work out. The landlord of that property said that he needed an answer right away, and that we would be locked into a one-year lease.

I drove to my wife's work and explained the situation. We either had to take the rental, or if we lost it, take a chance on our financer giving us the news we wanted to hear. The investor, Peter, knew we had a deadline, and told us that he would give us an answer on the day of the deadline. My wife, being the way she was, said, "You decide."

It was a tough decision. I know we wouldn't be on the

street either way as we were blessed with a support network, so I turned down the house we were going to rent, and for the first time, I prayed to God this way: "Hey there, God, I'm not sure what you're planning or doing, but we will be okay with whatever you decide, whether we get the church or not." When I say, "for the first time," I don't mean that it was my first prayer . . . but it was the first prayer I meant in my SOUL. I really meant that we would be OK, and we wouldn't be disappointed. And it wasn't just lip service; I didn't just say it in my mind, only to be disappointed if we didn't get the church. Did I want the church? Sure. But I guess for some reason the not caring, so to speak, struck me. It wasn't an "I don't care" attitude, but a sigh of relief. It was going to be decided one way or the other. It was a long year and a half, and we were in debt for it without even owning it.

With twenty-four hours left in the deadline, Peter agreed, and we got the church. It was truly unbelievable.

You may be saying, "Sure, it worked out in your favor this time, but what about another time when it didn't?" Since that occasion, I became acutely aware of my intentions in my soul, not my mind or ego. That was about seven years ago as of the writing of this book, and in that time, all I've been doing is concentrating on soul setting. I've given up on my mind/ego and the energy that I've freed up for my mind to create has been unbelievable. Many things have happened that, if I had my way, would have gone in a different direction. But they didn't, and guess what? I'm okay with the results because I HAVE TO BE.

I'd like to give you an example of when things didn't seem to work out. We're in real estate, and obviously I'd love to close every deal, but that's impossible. When a deal comes to us, I understand that if we're to be chosen to get this property, then we will, and if we don't, in my eyes, God is trying to protect me from something I can't see yet, and there will be another great property down the road. And there always is.

I guess the whole point of soul setting is to be patient and have faith that life is ALWAYS looking out for you, even if you can't see it at the time when you're going through it.

How Can All This Apply to Your Life?

Currently, if you're struggling, you know by now that you're resisting what's going on in your life. You don't like it, I understand, but for the most part, you can't control it. You no longer have a job because the company downsized or closed, you're getting divorced and you didn't want it to happen, someone close to you passed away, or any one of many other situations may have happened (remember, situations, not problems). Sure, you miss a loved one. Sure, you're scared about feeding the kids or keeping a roof over your head. We tend to constantly look at the outside world and compare it to the inside world, and the two clash so many times, but that's because of perception. We think (there goes your mind again) that the world should be a certain way when the way you think it should be is impossible.

The world can only be one way: the way it's going to go. When you get your soul setting in place correctly, it means understanding that the outside world functions independently of your inside world. You have very little control over the outside world. When you resist this fact, you'll constantly struggle—and far too many people struggle right to their grave. When you accept things are occurring the way they're going to, but not necessarily the way you think they should, you'll achieve a level of freedom that will energize you and give you a new life. Paying attention to this new energy will let you focus on things upon which you want to focus, such as physical health, relationships, and financial gain.

Exercise Time!

While driving, have you ever been running late, and it seems that you hit every red light? Do you know why that happens? Think of it this way: I believe that it's because you're sending out energy that you don't want a red light, but that energy doesn't understand wanting a red light or not wanting a red light. The energy can't differentiate between the two. You see, wherever you put your energy, that's usually where the energy goes. When you don't want a red light, you're putting your energy on a red light, so what appears? That's right: a red light. You get the red light that you were putting your energy on, and now you get even more angry because now you're running even later.

Try this instead:

Keep in mind that soul setting means not having a preference for results. When you approach a traffic signal, don't worry about it being red, even if you're late. After all, can you control the red light, or when it will appear? No, you can't. So, when you approach it, say to yourself, "It's okay, whatever color you want to be, you can be." Here's the key to the entire soul-setting concept: You have to really believe this in your soul and truly not care what color the traffic light stays or turns to. And yes, that means even if it makes you late to wherever you're going. You may say, "I really don't want it to turn red." Then go back to the ego, concentrate on that, and it *will* go red. All I'm asking is for you to understand the fundamental game for life is soul setting, and not mind setting.

Okay, so we're approaching the light, and if the light turns red, so be it—there's nothing I can do. Accept (notice I said "accept") that the light is red. If you get frustrated or angry, you've now shifted back to mind setting. If you've done your soul setting properly, you won't get mad, and you'll accept this red light. And how does this change our state of being late? It doesn't. Because the lights are the situation; your time management is the issue. Leave earlier next time, and you won't be late. Now that we have time management under control, driving amongst the red lights will no longer be an issue.

So now that we're not late anymore, who here likes red lights? Nobody—even if you're not late and you have time to sit at red lights. The same principles apply, however, except now that you're not late, this will be easier. You're approaching a traffic signal, accepting that it might turn red, and you're okay with that. Whatever color it stays or turns, you will accept. If it turns red, that's okay, because now you have time to look around and enjoy the day. Obviously, if it stays green, you'll accept that as well and enjoy your day even more. Your preference doesn't change, because remember, you have no preference.

When your energy is on your ego results and not your soul results, that's when we get into trouble. When that happens, the outside world often doesn't match your inside world. Not having a preference for what color light you get, versus what light you'll actually get, are two different things.

I very seldom run late, but when I do, I still apply this "red-light theory," and I don't care what color light I get, because if I am late, again, that's my time-management issue, not a red-light issue. By not having a preference anytime, it seems like I get green lights most of the time. It's crazy. My energy isn't focused on a red light; it's focused on "any color is good with me." Remember, getting angry at a red light means that you haven't accepted the traffic signal's color in your soul—you're still in your ego. Accepting life on its terms is the key. When you resist, you struggle.

After you do this exercise for a week, email me with your thoughts. I would love to hear from you, and if you're still struggling with this exercise, maybe we can help.

> **Thoughts are generated from the soul.**
>
> / Levy /

To Believe or Not Believe in Goal Setting

Contrary to what you may have heard or been taught, my belief is that goal setting sets you up for failure and disappointment. How many times have you set a goal, say in weight loss or money saving, and not obtained it?

When you live life through soul setting, you enjoy life and there are no goals. Instead of having a goal, simply live with purpose and intent. As each month goes by, you know in your soul if you're doing better or not. Your improvement will be noticed.

Goal setting is rooted in external outcomes. What happens if you don't reach your goal? How do you feel? Defeated—and chances are for a lot of people, some form

---

If you set your goals so ridiculously high and it's a failure, you will fail above everyone else's success

/ James Cameron /

of depression and/or anxiety may creep in. If your goal is financial in nature, don't think that you can know whether you'll be ahead financially in three months or a year. As with anything in this world, something always comes up, and if you have a goal and that something comes up to disrupt you, then these circumstances can be negative. If you focus on your intention instead of your goals, then your daily intention can easily be redirected back when unforeseen circumstances pop up.

Here's the thing: You know where you want to go, but you don't know how to get there. I'll use an example from my life. Up until the age of fifty, I was trying vision boards, manifestations, laws of attraction, and any combination of these things for more than thirty years. At fifty, I discovered that I was trying too hard to have my life controlled by outside forces. When things didn't go right, I would get very angry. I didn't understand that life was going to unfold in front of me the way it wanted to instead of unfolding the way I wanted it to. This was a pivotal realization, and once I had it, a massive change occurred. As I grew into soul setting, I could see changes in me over the next few months, and as the years went by, my original goals were being realized. I always wanted to get into new home building—and it only took more than twelve years to do it. New home building is very expensive before you even put a shovel in the ground, and I never had the money, nor could I obtain it from investors.

When I discovered soul setting, goal setting went out

the window for me. I realized that if I was going to gain any ground in life, I had to do it from *inside* of me. This is how life works, and for the first time, I could see the power of conquering the inside of me versus the outside of me. Letting go of power, of control, was very new to me. I decided to give life a chance to run my life, instead of trying to control it myself. Suddenly, stress was lifted from my mind and my body. My health changed, and for the better. Anger was different for me. Sure, I still got mad now and then, but it was a long way from the temper tantrums that I used to have. Are my anger issues gone? No. But my bouts of temper only last a few minutes, and now when things don't go right according to my mind, I can recognize it and move on without the tantrums (for the most part). When will these brief spells of anger come to an end completely? Who cares? Remember—stop caring.

And when I say, "stop caring," I don't mean, "Who cares who I hurt in the meantime?" or "In the meantime, I'll be selfish and do whatever I want." It means, "Who cares what life brings me, because I can handle it." Understanding life will continue to bring forward that which I need to work on from the inside.

How Do You Know It's In Your Soul and Not Your Ego?

This part of soul setting is the easiest to understand in theory. But to practice it—a practice that will last a lifetime—can be tremendously rewarding when mastered.

Let me tell you another story: My daughter just celebrated her twenty-eighth birthday. I sent her a text, but this wasn't any normal text. It read: "Well, I understand happy birthday is in order. Twenty-eight years ago, you started your journey. For some of it, it hasn't been easy, but it is what happened for yourself to become you. You will continue to grow through good and bad experiences, and the way you deal with them is up to you and only you. ALWAYS here for you to lend an ear and an opinion. Love ya, Ash."

Her response? "Thank you."

I can remember reading that text, and thinking about where I was up to that date. It was another one of those "ah-ha" moments for me.

I had really put my soul into the words I was speaking to her—sort of a father/daughter moment in which I felt that God was sending me the words I was writing to her. Yes, I was arrogant enough to have been impressed with the wisdom I was sending her on her birthday. And when I received those two little words back, "thank you," it burnt a hole in my heart, and I could feel my temperature rising inside.

The response I was expecting from her was something more like, "Wow, Dad, I love those words of encouragement." But I didn't get that. I got, "Thank you." As I gazed upon those words and felt myself getting upset, I caught myself. This is exactly what soul setting is, and how it can transform your life. I was getting caught up in what I call, "The inside doesn't match the outside concept."

The soul didn't match the ego, and I caught it. As I was sitting there starting to smile and relax, I realized that I didn't know what my daughter was doing at the time of her response. She could have just cut herself with a knife while cooking, or she could have been in the middle of laundry or grocery shopping or any other number of things that didn't match her true feelings at the time. Then again, it could have been her true feelings, and my words weren't as magical to her as they were to me. Either way, I had to learn to accept her feelings and her response. After all, that response was based on her conditioning and her life for the past twenty-eight years. Her experiences may have been telling her to hold back, as she was just going through a rough break-up with her partner.

I had to accept her response as it was: "Thank you." I had to accept what she had said in its simplicity—maybe a genuine thank you, maybe not. I accepted it, and life was good again.

When my daughter reacted with her "thank you" to my text and I felt myself getting upset, I caught myself. I thought about her life instead of my life, and what she may have gone through, something that I knew very little about. I thought about how her experiences have created her identity. When I started to think about this, I relaxed, and I just breathed. Everything was going to be okay, I thought.

I can remember saying to myself, "How could you be so righteous in thinking those words were gospel?" I also thought, "Why did I think this way? What did I want in return for my words of wisdom?" My ego said, "You wanted to be put up on a pedestal and regarded as a saint."

What was I thinking?

Remember, rule number one: Never expect anything in return.

Bingo. There was my answer. I expected my ego to be stroked with a brilliant comeback that would soothe my insecurity.

Why? Well, that's too easy. Look into one's past environment or experiences, and there were very few words of encouragement. Perhaps that kept me wanting my ego stroked whenever I thought I came up with a clever line. End of story.

As you can see, soul setting can be easy to understand, but difficult to master. As each day grows, you will continue on your way to a liberation of the mind the likes of which you never thought was even possible.

The story I just told is an example of how arguments start. After all, what is an argument? An argument is a disagreement about a particular subject that two people are discussing—two people who have completely different views on a topic.

And what happens? The egos of both people are being challenged, and for both people in the argument, the inside word doesn't match the outside world. In other words, what one person *thinks* is happening, isn't happening. The other person doesn't agree with what you are saying based on their conditioning as a child and their identity. Yelling ensues, and each arguer challenges the other in their quests to prove the other wrong. Now, each is locked in a battle to convince the other that he or she is right.

Everyone Is Right

Get this: Everyone is right. About everything. That's right, everyone's opinion about anything is right, and no one is wrong. Nobody is wrong.

How can that be?

Think about it. When we argue, the ego always wants to be right. It needs and wants things. The soul never needs to be right and is always understanding with regards to the way things are at any given moment. If you can draw closer to that soul, then the drama you're currently experiencing will subside. Your stress will diminish. Of course, that doesn't mean you have to be a doormat. When it comes to everyday casual conversation, you can discuss topics in which your opinion might be different than that of others. But you can simply drop the matter and understand that according to their own mind and ego, they're right as well.

Do you ever argue with the people with whom you have relationships? Of course you do. But why? It's because each side is trying to convince the other that he or she is wrong. The ego *always* wants to be right. It needs and wants to be right. The soul never needs to be right and is always understanding of the way things are. It knows that at any given moment, the way things are is okay just the way it is, because it *is just the way it is.* **IT JUST IS.**

Here's an example of how both people can be right. Let's say you're talking about discipline in schools in the seventies. One person argues that the school system went to pot when they removed the strap for discipline. The strap was usually a leather belt that was slapped across your hands by the principal for doing something wrong, like stealing. I myself was on the wrong end of the strap for stealing three marbles that were on the teacher's desk. Then, after the punishment at school, the principal would call the parents, and in many cases, the parents would say, "If you get the strap at school, be prepared to get the strap at home, too." And I did. Do you think I ever stole again?

But back to the example. One person in this argument is for the strap system in school, and the other person is against it. They begin to discuss the system and why it might or might not have had any merit. Whichever side you may be on, you're trying to convince the person on the other side that they're wrong. But are they?

Why do you think your opinion is correct and the other person's is wrong? Usually, it's based on the values and morals that have been passed down to you. Maybe when you were a child, the disciplinary action your parents took was some form of spanking with an object. In that case, you took that form of discipline as the best one to correct a child's behavior. Perhaps the other person didn't get punished that way; instead, he or she was grounded for a few days. This person doesn't see the need for physical punishment based on the morals and values with which they were raised.

Morals and values can get even broader than this. Parents' values are passed on from generation to generation, so are those of the friends you used to hang out with. Chances are they are very close to your values. If you don't believe in stealing and thought that it was wrong, chances are you didn't have close friends that stole, either.

In most cases, when you find yourself in a heated discussion—or even a discussion that has devolved into a full-blown argument—stop. Become aware of your emotions. Breathe. Look at the topic at hand. Does it fall into the category of one in which both sides are right based on their developmental history? Or is it something that needs to be discussed more responsibly?

Relationships can be easy if you understand this concept. Now, I'm not asking you to be a doormat and accept this principle every time you have a discussion with someone. However, if you start to become aware of conversations that you're in with your partner, spouse, co-workers, strangers, etc., and the first thing you feel is the urge to defend your position, remember that EVERYONE IS RIGHT. This simple concept will help increase your empathy and your emotional intelligence, and that will spill over into your career, and your chances of success will increase, as well.

The Outside World Doesn't Match My Inside World

One of the best philosophies you can adopt while soul setting is that your outside world seldom matches your inside world. Think about it: why do we struggle and create drama? Why do we argue with people? Often, it's because we're being defensive about our stand on a subject and we think that our opinion is correct. We defend it and we work to convince the other person that he or she is wrong. This is the mind/ego at its best.

We each have an ego that has adopted principles and perceptions through years of experience, and through a lifetime of teachings of values, beliefs, and morals from our parents, teachers, friends, and everyone around us. Some of these beliefs can be abstract and not conducive to our overall growth as a human being. This is why we argue. Our ego never likes to be wrong.

Delusion versus Reality

Earlier, I quoted Napoleon Hill's famous saying, "Whatever your mind can conceive and believe, it can achieve." This quote is misleading. We raise our children with this notion, and when we do, we set them up for disappointment. It's impossible to be anything you want. There are realistic limitations. And yes, I'm well aware of creating limitations that will sabotage your dreams; however, running a four-minute mile when you're not physically able can be a stumbling block.

Everyone on Earth is here for a purpose, and that is to serve one another with passion. When we look at passion, it should be something that you want to wake up with to start the day. You're energized by it, and when you have it, time flies by incredibly quickly.

Let's look at the Wright Brothers, who invented human flight. Their father bought them a miniature helicopter powered by an elastic, and the boys started making duplicates of these helicopters. The Wright brothers were also in the bicycle business, which they worked while admiring flight. With the inspiration of the bicycle being controlled on the ground, they had to develop balance of an airplane in the air. That balance had to be controlled by someone on that plane: a pilot.

The Wright brothers had a natural desire for learning, and they were self-employed at a young age. Invention was in their blood, and the list of inventions they created is mind-boggling (I encourage you to Google their history). Since human flight hadn't been accomplished yet, the Wright brothers had a basic knowledge of balance and what it took to invent products. There was no delusion on the part of the Wright brothers, they knew deep in their soul they could eventually conquer the prospect of flight, and as you know, they did. If you were to ask them to paint or sing, they probably wouldn't be able to do so, and they didn't pursue those careers because that's not where their passions lied.

Let's fast forward to today. Yes, there are still inventions that aren't invented yet, and someone will have to invent them. However, look with caution into your soul and find out if these inventions will serve humankind and whether you're looking at these inventions as a way to obtain financial gain. If you're looking solely at the financial aspects of doing something, then your chances of success drop immediately, and your prospects of failure are very high indeed.

Soul setting is based on reality, on your natural gifts, on what you find easy to comprehend and execute when others find the same tasks difficult or impossible. Usually, these gifts can be found at a young age. Your gift is something you think about often over the years. Your gift will not create depression or anxiety, as it comes easily, and you enjoy doing it. Being aware of your gift will have a profound effect on your life.

Understanding Others

Soul setting can be a huge advantage in life for anyone who understands and uses this philosophy and continues to develop it. As you develop soul setting, your identity changes in a positive way. Your stress level decreases, as does the drama in which you continuously find yourself.

As we've discussed, having the "everyone is right" attitude can go a long way. We've discussed how arguments start. When one person's relationship with an idea is all he or she believes, and you believe in a contrary idea, each of you somehow needs to prove you're right. Ta-da! An argument starts.

If only we could read other people's minds, or even go back in time to see where they came up with their version of what's right. If you could understand how you became who you are, then that might help you to understand how others became who they are.

When you were younger, your parents raised you the best they could with what they knew and instilled in you beliefs and their versions of right and wrong. Each belief system is handed down from generation to generation. That, of course, doesn't mean each generation is right, but at that time and to that person, it seemed right.

As humans, we have the right to choose what we believe. Take racism, for example. Do you really believe racist people were born that way? Of course not. Someone had to teach these people those concepts. As those people grew and were part of their parents' environment, they were probably around other people who shared the parents' point of view, and it became part of them. Can you blame the parents? You could, but they were taught those concepts from *their* parents, and so on.

As humans, we should be evolving into better humans—remember, that's one of our purposes, to grow spiritually. As adults, if everyone grew spiritually and understood each other and how they became who they are, we would all be more compassionate towards each other.

When you become an adult, it's YOUR responsibility to grow and to learn. As you grow and learn other concepts, you might learn that your parents' views are wrong for you, so you change as a person, and you do not become a racist. When you have children, you perhaps will not raise them with the views of racism. This is how we can break the chain of views.

When I come across someone whose anger seems to be a basic character trait, I confront them with nothing but compassion. If you actually sit with the idea of what kind of terrible past they must have lived through, you can become sympathetic towards that person as a fellow human being. You can begin to understand that they don't have to be that way. But again, a huge percentage of the world will go to their graves not understanding each other, and more importantly, not understanding themselves.

As humans, it's easy to fall prey to our egos. We always want to be right. We're constantly trying to convince or change the other person's mind.

Stop doing this.

Again, the majority of what we struggle with will not matter in two weeks, let alone ten years. Sit with yourself and think about what's going on. Are you thinking as a victim of circumstance?

For example, if only I wasn't raised in a broken family, if only I had more money, if only that person didn't behave that way, or finally (and this is the big one), if only that terrible thing didn't happen to me, things would be so different.

These examples are easy to use as they put the blame on someone or something else and can give us an explanation that basically boils down to, "I was just at the wrong place at the wrong time." First, there's no such thing as the wrong place. Nothing happens at the wrong time, even terrible things. I call anything that happens "a divine appointment." Everything in this world is already figured out.

Things are going to happen, terrible things and glorious things. And how do I know? BECAUSE THEY HAPPEN. And these things, the brutal things and the wonderful things and everything in between, happen to both people who deserve them and people who don't. These things JUST ARE. The Masterful Creator knows why people go through what they go through. It's to grow spiritually. Each of us has to go through our own suffering to get to a point where we know that we need to look at our inner self and stop looking at the outer self. This is the only way to live in peace and liberation of the mind. That's when the struggle has a chance to subside. Many people never see that, and they continue forever down the path of victimhood.

My Definition of Success

Success for me is having inner peace and freedom, where my mind isn't cluttered with drama and things I can't control, and understanding the world and my ability to do what I want, when I want.

If my truck needs repairs, I can't just go get it fixed without the financial worry of where the money is going to come from to do it. If you don't think financial outlook is a key factor for success, you must be kidding yourself. I know a lot of gurus that say that money doesn't buy you happiness, and I agree (to a point). Let's face it, you need money to pay the bills, and to buy food, shelter, and clothes. Everything else is just materialistic items you don't really need: the Rolex, the dream vacation, jewelry, the flashy car, etc. Sure, it would be nice to have these things, but remember, the purpose of life is to help everyone and to grow spiritually inside.

By developing intentions rather than goals, you set yourself up to respond to circumstances you didn't expect versus reacting. Reacting tends to create stress. Setting goals is fixating on the future, and we're not in the future yet, so why worry about something that hasn't happened? If you focus on habits, discipline, and consistency, your chances of success are greatly increased, because there are no goals to focus on that create disappointment if they're not met.

I'm not telling you to live a life of complacency. I'm saying, live life at the moment and enjoy each second of the day. Live for now, not future goals. Goals are usually out of our control. They're based on outside factors that have to be perfect. Life gets in the way of your goals every time. For example, writing this book was daunting, at least in the beginning. So, I broke it down daily, and wrote every day. And yes, it took three years to write, but I didn't look at it as daunting. I looked at it as if my great-great-grandchild was going to read it one day. That's it. Every day, I wrote something, and it got completed. Every day, I worked on myself and the contentment that each day gave me. I worked hard each day, and yes, if I didn't feel like working hard, I didn't. I never felt guilty about not working. This didn't happen very often, as I developed good habits in writing, or looking for opportunities in the real estate world, or even just something little, like smiling at ten people a day.

> **When you give your mind a voice,
> it becomes your identity.**
>
> / Levy /

Problems

What would you think if I told you that nobody has problems? That's right, nobody!

Come on, I hear you saying. *What about the person who just wrecked her car? What about the person who can't pay his rent and is about to be evicted from his apartment? What about the parents who just lost their young child?* And the list goes on.

No, these aren't problems. We as humans are conditioned to look at the negative side of circumstances and situations. It's about perspective. When your soul is set and you start to live life through your soul and not your mind or ego, these so-called problems will change.

So how do you get through these situations and circumstances? You begin by thinking about anything you're going through as just that: a circumstance or situation. NOT a problem. Let's look at an example:

**It's not the problem that causes us the suffering;
it's our thinking about the problem.**

/ Byron Katie /

You're about to lose your house or get kicked out of your apartment. How did this occur? When looking back at that lost job, why did you lose your job? Sometimes it's our own responsibility. We were late a lot, we didn't get our work done on time, whatever. Most of the time, though, it's nothing in our control. Times are tough, they had to lay off people, and you had no control over this. So, what happens? You get behind on payments, you blame other people and your bad luck, and you begin to create negative energy.

It's simple, really. Life doesn't make mistakes. And even though going through a certain situation or circumstance may absolutely suck, this is where the most growth in your life can occur. Take a look at something that happened poorly. During that time, it could have been devastating, simply because you looked at it that way. It was through your ego. Changing the lens you look through is the difference between resisting and struggling or becoming free and at peace.

Another thing to consider: You are put on this Earth to have a great life. For me, God didn't want me to struggle, He wanted me to spiritually grow, and that doesn't mean religion, it means peace of mind and liberation. You have two choices: a life of personal struggle or a life of personal growth. Remember, our purpose here in this world is not to struggle. Everyone's purpose is the same. We are here to spiritually grow and contribute to each other. That's it. It doesn't matter what you're going through, whether you lost a limb in an accident or got that huge raise and promotion, life is going to happen the way it's going to happen.

Looking at your life as though you're a victim versus a contributor can keep you in a "Why me?" mode and in a state of constant struggle. When you look from an outside view, and the world isn't going according to your inside view, you will constantly resist life as it is. Being this way is delusional, and not realistic. My life has not gone even close to the way I thought it would go, but I'm grateful, and due to my views and spiritual growth, I now have zero depression, suicidal thoughts, and anxiety.

How?

Having dealt with overwhelming depression and anxiety to the point of planning my own suicide more than once, I'm familiar with therapy. I went for years each week to get help, and I recall during my last trip, the doctor saying to me, "Levy, you understand you will more than likely have to learn to deal with this depression, don't you?"

"What do you mean, 'deal with it'?" I asked.

"You'll probably have some form of depression for the rest of your life," he said. "Your depression at best will be mild but will creep up from time to time. But good news is with medication and some simple techniques, you can cope with depression and have a somewhat normal life."

Then and there, I thought to myself, "NO WAY am I going to deal with this for the rest of my life." After all, I had probably had fifty or sixty years of my life yet to live.

I walked out and never went back.

This was an "ah ha!" moment for me. It was time for me to figure out what was going on, and how I was going to rid myself of this depression. After all, I didn't want to cope with it for the rest of my life, I wanted it GONE.

And so, my quest began. I began to do research and tried to teach myself how to get rid of this terrible mental issue. The first thing I wanted to do was to wean myself off my medication. Although I certainly don't recommend this for everyone, it was what I felt I had to do. In my case, I really felt in my soul that I didn't need to be on them. That was more than fifteen years ago. I carried on with my life, and yes, I had depression from time to time, and yes, it was still difficult.

During this time, I was still drinking, and during my journey, without even realizing it, I replaced the pills with more drinking. I became an everyday drinker, and sometimes I would just sit in front of the computer all day, drinking. I was working at the time, but it was a midnight shift in a factory, and I got to work by myself in a huge office. I did quality control for steel bearings, and I really enjoyed it. I changed shifts with my coworkers (no one liked the midnight shift), and it gave me a chance to drink during the day. It also gave me the chance to work the shift when the management and bosses weren't around.

"The implicit assumption behind any goal is this: 'Once I reach my goal, then I'll be happy.' The problem with a goals-first mentality is that you're continuing putting off happiness until the next milestone." —James Clear

I've spent more than thirty years of my adult life goal setting. Here are some examples of the goals I didn't reach at the end of a year:

- Paying off certain loans
- Purchasing ten houses
- Reaching a financial goal

Losing a certain amount of weight

Obtain a certain physique

If your definition of success (and this was my definition for fifty years) was to be a zillionaire, you'll not get there ninety-nine percent of the time. This isn't what your soul requires; your soul requires growth. I've noticed that when I stopped caring about that need to be a zillionaire, and really meant it in my soul and not just my mind, things changed quickly.

In the last five years, our family's financial picture has changed. We've been able to donate money to the causes we love and still have money left over. We can fix our vehicles whenever we need to and not worry about where the money is going to come from. We can go to the grocery store and simply buy the food we enjoy without worrying about going to the cashier and wondering what we'll need to put back because we just don't have enough money.

Do we go on elaborate vacations? Nope, but that's because I don't like vacations. I really, really love what I do, so for me, it's like a vacation.

Forgiveness

Let's talk about your past . . . and perhaps your present.

Up until now, you've been doing your best you can to survive. But you're struggling. Before this book, you might not have known that *you don't have to struggle*. You can learn to be present and live in the now, at this exact moment, and enjoy your life for the gift that it is.

Let's look at your upbringing. Like you, your parents were likely doing the best they could while raising you with what they knew at the time. Whatever their faults might have been, they were doing the best they could, and if they could have become better individuals, chances are they would have.

When you look at your current life, up to this point, you didn't know there was a different way to live. And it's useless to forgive yourself because you did the best you could with what you knew. What is there to forgive? Shame and guilt have no place for residency in your mind.

I hear so many people saying things like, "I have forgiven my mother or father," or "I have let go." The way I see it, things that have happened, have happened, and *that's it*. It happened. Let's move on.

Have you ever said to yourself, "Man, with what I know today, if I could go back and do it all over again . . ." Well, you can't. In time, you'll be able to look back at your difficult situations and realize they were exactly why you are where you are today.

Let's look at what bothers you in your mind. What creates conflict or struggle? Is it relationships? Your job? Finances? Any or all of these might have hit a nerve with some readers, because from time to time we all struggle with one or more of these.

Let's look at relationships, whether they be with a spouse, a romantic companion, a friend, or a co-worker. Why are these relationships difficult? Chances are your outside world doesn't match your inside world, and people are just driving you nuts based on their view or their perspective of life, or a particular topic you're arguing about.

What if I suggest that you take on a perspective that says, "Everyone is right" (we discussed the merits of this concept earlier). There are two ways to think about life. When you're constantly struggling in relationships (or anything from your past or present, for that matter), are you considering yourself to be a victim of circumstance, or a victim of programming?

When people behave the way they do, it's usually because of programming. Their belief and value systems are perhaps different from yours because of the way they were brought up. This is usually passed down from generation to generation. That doesn't make it a correct way to live, however. As generations are raised, they're brought up the way the generations before them have been raised. They simply didn't know any other way.

As each generation moves forward, so do their values and belief systems. You don't have to look far to see this. Use racism, for example. Racists aren't born racists. Someone has to teach them to think that way. The only way out of this programming is to become self-aware and have one of those "ah-ha!" moments that perhaps awaken people to a deeper meaning of life.

You might ask yourself (as countless others have asked before you), "Isn't there more to life than this?" But you should go one step beyond asking that question. You should go out and seek what more life has to offer. This is what I hope this book does for you. So, the answer to that question is to become self-aware, to become more aware of your surroundings, to notice what you take in through all of your five senses. What are you telling yourself? How do you react to every situation? And most of all, can you accept your life as it is now. Now is maybe all you have left. Be present in the now. Never cope or obtain techniques just to survive life through substances or medications (although, there are cases when you may be required to take medication to get back into the now). You don't want to survive life; you want to thrive in life. Never chase anything; let life evolve. That doesn't mean you don't have to go get it. It just means that if it comes to you, awesome. If it doesn't, it doesn't mean it won't. Never chase relationships, money, sales, or happiness.

You really must get this part into your soul, and it can be difficult. The "I don't care" attitude towards your future goes a long way. Of course, this doesn't mean that you sit in front of the TV and eat a bag of chips and drink a beer and think, "Levy said to just stop caring and what I want will come to me like a manifestation." This isn't what I'm talking about. You have to work hard without expectation. Yes, *without expectation*. Continue to work in the field you really enjoy and one that you would do for free. As I write this book, I really enjoy helping others, and look forward to the day someone comes to me and says, "I'm so glad you pointed me in a different direction." Now, if that happens, great. And if it doesn't happen, that's okay as well.

You see, I don't care. I know deep in my soul that this book will help because it's what I love to do. I have zero stress when I talk about my passion for soul setting—it gives me kind of a rush. My fifty years of life experience—my failure after failure, massive depression, anxiety, fear, financial distress, failed marriage, and the list goes on and on—has allowed me to seek a better life, just the way you're doing. I'm grateful for everything I've gone through because if I hadn't gone through it, I wouldn't be here writing this book and helping you.

We respond to every little situation positively or negatively, and as we do so negatively, we deplete our energy. By letting go of situations that we can't handle, we build up positive energy to a point of absolute pleasure. The next time someone, or some situation, sets you off, stop. Breathe. Say to yourself, "Is this going to affect me in six months?" Then ask, "Is this a conflict between my outside world versus my inside world? Chances are in most cases, the daily barrage of circumstances and situations are a conflict. You think, "Jeez, why am I getting so angry?" It's because you didn't think the situation was fair, and it conflicts with what you think it should be, or how others should be behaving. Sorry, but life doesn't work that way. Being self-aware and breathing before reacting will increase your positive energy and your output in life.

Quitting

I get sick and tired of people telling me to never quit on my dreams and goals.

To me, the idea of never quitting on your goals is hogwash. I see so many people on the wrong path, and they wonder why they're full of stress, depression, and anxiety when things aren't going their way. I think back to my numerous attempts at multi-level marketing (MLM) that

I thought were the golden ticket to get me out of the mountain of crap I was buried in. They never worked out for me. Most of them were attempted when I was a lot younger, and some I had to pay money to get involved with (Important lesson: Anytime you have to pay someone to get into a job, or get into a sales organization, RUN. Never pay to get involved).

When I joined these companies, it was usually out of desperation and greed. I was down on my luck, and I didn't have very much money. If you look at your own life, doesn't that make sense? How many of your financial decisions are made from desperation? Many of the decisions are wrong, but you have just enough hope in them to buy in. The next thing you know, you're at a meeting, and boom, you're in.

Which brings me back to quitting. My philosophy is that it's okay to quit if you're going in the wrong direction. "But how do I know if I'm going in the wrong direction?" you may ask. This part is so easy.

If you wake up every day with no motivation, or dreading to get up to face the day, that's a sure-fire way to know you're on the wrong path.

Too many people think financially. I know it's difficult not to—after all, money pays the bills, and you can't get the stuff you need and want without it. Other people may argue that they have hundreds (or even thousands) of dollars tied up in a business venture—thinking, *I just can't quit now. I have too much to lose.*

Don't you realize, however, that you have too much to lose if you stay? I've seen people quit what they had been doing for more than ten years and start on the path they should have been on in the first place. Usually, this correct path is more in line with their talents and what they love to do, and within a short amount of time, they are financially past where they were. Their stress level is down, and they're content with many happy moments in life.

They are people who love to start their day.

No Preferences

One of the most profound concepts that I'm working on is, "Having no Preference." That is to say, if I were going to get a job, I understand that God is setting me up for great things. Does this include nailing the job interview? Of course it does. However, if I get this job, great. But if I don't get it, it's okay because there are greater things ahead for me.

Now, the preference for most of us would be to get the job—maybe it has a better salary, or a better location. It's only natural to have a preference to get the job. When you go in with this attitude, it sends a negative tone. Ask yourself, "Can I be okay with what's going on right now?" You have no choice but to accept it because it is going on. Resist it and you will struggle, and that's where most humans live: the struggling mode. Because things inside your mind don't match what's going on with the outside world.

STORY TIME

My wife and I purchase houses and either flip them or hang onto them for investment purposes. Years ago (and I'm talking years ago), I would bid on a house, and preference would be, "I need this." I would need the house I bid on so badly that it would consume me. More times than not, I wouldn't get the house, and I'd go into a deep, dark place. Depression. It would last for days.

Today, I don't have a preference when we put a bid in on a house because I really believe God is looking out for me. I can't see the mold behind the walls in the house I bid on and lost; I can't see the wiring that needed to be replaced—not to mention the asbestos I can't see. Today, if I don't get a property, I simply give gratitude to God and thank him for saving me something terrible that I can't see. I always know there is going to be another great house for me, and guess what? There is. Please apply this to your life, and you will tend to obtain more than you don't get.

Here's the thing, though, you have to have no preference in your soul and not in your mind/ego. If you truly don't have a preference and that's what you feel deep in your soul, when you don't get it, then you're truly okay with it. You have zero stress or frustration. You understand you're being protected, and something better is coming.

Don't Be Attached to Your Results!

When you look beyond today, you have the tendency to create stress. You will analyze why you aren't where you think you should be. There we go again, thinking with our minds about success. Let's use the example that everyone seems to want to go to, and that is being a millionaire. We tend to look at the feeling of becoming a millionaire and what it can do for you, which is the fallacy of becoming happy.

Happiness is an emotion and not a state of being. Never chase happiness. Become complacent. Not in the manner of becoming a doormat, but rather in the sense of just sitting back and doing nothing and accepting what life brings to you. When you engage in the daunting task of gaining a million dollars, it can seem impossible. Believe it or not, today is the best time to create a million dollars out of any era in history. But as with any big result that you wish to accomplish, you must first believe it in your soul, and not your mind/ego. You must have discipline, consistency, and patience. Remember, as discussed in the financial section, it's what you do with your money on a regular basis that will create the financial outcome you seek. When your mind goes into the future, a future that you aren't even in yet, and you create emotions for that future, you're creating a resistance that you can't see, or that you're not aware of. It took me until I was fifty years old to find this out. I finally let go of the future and concentrated on the NOW. Evidently, this is the key to creating what you want: a lack of care about the future. Accepting the now for what it is, and not forcing your future, will assist in a more relaxed lifestyle.

This accepting life as it comes has affected every aspect of my life, especially when it comes to my financial life. I continue to work hard, and opportunities just seem to appear. Keep in mind that I've worked hard for years, just in a different way: not looking too far into the future.

STORY TIME

I've been in real estate for more than twenty years, buying properties, changing the design of the kitchen from one area of the room to another side of the house, taking load-bearing walls down to make it an open concept, and so on (I like to think I taught Jonathan and Drew Scott, the Property Brothers, this concept). I even started before HGTV got its start in the renovation business. In my drinking years, I can remember seeing a house for sale for $60,000 and thinking, "This one is my golden ticket! This will solve all my financial woes!"

I remember one particular house especially well. Three other people were bidding on it. I badly wanted this property. And this is where you may identify with my situation: I didn't get this house. I remember going into my basement at the time—it was small and had a low ceiling with a fireplace, TV, and a very comfortable couch. I didn't take the news of not getting the property well, and I sank into depression. I suffered from severe depression at the time, and often I would literally stop my life for three to five days and just drink. And drink. And drink some more.

I wonder if some of you can relate to this to some degree? Not getting that apartment, or that job, or the date with that special someone. Anyway, after those three to five days, I would realize that I can't do this forever. I would go on repeating that behavior for years, never getting anywhere.

Fast-forward to the present. I have soul setting in place pretty well now. I certainly have more work, but in this time of life and a peaceful state of mind, I'm miles ahead of where I used to be. I'm still in the real estate market, I still buy properties, and we now build, as well. When a gold mine shows up, I simply put it in my soul that I would love to have it. The only difference now is that I don't set my heart on it. That's the key: not setting my heart on it. And this is difficult. I say to myself, I would love this opportunity, and if I get it, great. But if I don't get it, that's great, too.

This part of soul setting is difficult, but when you continue to practice it, your life creates different opportunities. As a result, I've taken a different perspective on getting properties like these. And you can, too. If you're trying to get a job, an apartment, a car, a man or woman, or anything else, change your perspective. Look to your higher power. As I mentioned, my higher power is God. He's always looking out for me. Life isn't doing things to me, it is doing things FOR me. Whether it's situations or circumstances that I don't like, in the long run, life is trying to teach me something.

When I don't get a property that I want, I say to myself (through my higher power), "Thank you for not giving me this situation. I'm guessing there's asbestos in the walls or mold that I can't see, or something else on a long, long list of problems. I can move on quickly now, and there is absolutely no depression or alcohol necessary to get past it."

How do you know if you're doing this correctly? How do you know that it's in your soul and not your ego? Easy. If you can move on without that apartment, or that car, or that potential romantic partner, and you're not disappointed and you can accept things the way they are because IT JUST IS, then you've done it right. You don't get depressed or fixated on the lack of result you received. You move on. If you get depressed or upset, then it wasn't in your soul, it was in your ego, and it's time to work on it some more. Not having a desire for a result is difficult, and admittedly I still struggle from time to time, as will you. After all, we're all human, and we have to give ourselves a break.

Pain is life's lesson for promotion.

/ Levy /

Why People Struggle

This is my favorite thing to talk about because so many of us struggle in life. We struggle with our health, our finances, our relationships, and even with our spirituality. Struggling creates stress, and let's face it, stress kills. Not right away, but over time—maybe a couple of years, or a few decades, but eventually, stress has a multitude of effects on the body, from blood pressure to heart troubles to even problems with addiction. In my case, during the years when I was struggling, I became an alcoholic, and my depression was so severe that I was planning my own suicide. Pile on top of that a heaping helping of anxiety, and it seemed that I was doomed.

The situation that you're in can be attributed to the decisions you've made in the past. These decisions were made with what you knew at the time. Take our parents, for example. Frequently, we look at the decisions our parents made, and we realize that they were poor decisions. Maybe

---

Strength and growth come only through continuous effort and struggle.

/ Napoleon Hill /

they were, maybe they weren't. Either way, they were decisions made with what our parents knew through their own upbringing, their environment, and the way they perceived life and the future.

You see, there is a difference between WANTS and NEEDS, and this is exactly what I'm talking about when I discuss mind setting versus soul setting.

Mind setting is usually related to dream fulfillment. It has to do with your WANTS. We look into the future for validation, and we compare our outside world to others. What do others have that I don't have, but want? Do they have the BMW, the Rolex, the vacation home, etc. We are built to live in the mind, the ego, and that's where so many people go to die, never really obtaining what they need: peace and freedom of the mind.

If you ask anyone what they want, they can usually tell you, but peace and freedom of the mind is rarely up there on people's bucket list. Yet, if you ask them, "Would you like to live a life free of stress, a life where your relationships with others thrive and there is little to no drama," you know what they'll say. I've never met someone who says, "Nah, I'm good, I enjoy the stress."

Why is it then that we don't put this on our bucket list and make it a goal for our lives? It's because our ego won't let us, and we really don't pay any attention to our soul. Sure, from time to time it may creep into a conversation, maybe when someone says something like, "Man, I'm so sick of my life being nothing but constant pressure!" This is usually where the conversation grinds to a halt because no one wants to hear your bellyaching.

Soul setting is a one-man show. We talk to others about

soul setting, and bells and whistles go off in their head. They think, "This person must be nuts." They imagine hours of meditation, voodoo dolls, and gowns that we wear while we pace the room, chanting affirmations. It's really a turn-off for so many.

Soul setting isn't anything like this. It's simply a self-awareness of something realistic, and not delusional. We tend to live in a delusion, thinking everything is cool, everything is great, when it's not. You see, we live two different lives. One life is outside, in public, and we are fake on the outside and look happy. But when we get within our own four walls, things take a different twist. This isn't living—it's dying.

Why do this when there's an alternative?

How to Get There and Where to Start?

Breathe. It's just that simple. Become aware of your surroundings and adopt a different perspective that's different from that of the crowd around you.

You're ready to stop living a life that's common among your fellow humans.

You're not going to be a slave to outside media.

You're ready for a life that's lived from the inside, which is something we can all do, even though many go to their graves not understanding this, and they live a life of constant struggle instead. If only they spent as much time on their inner environment as they do on the outside environment, life would be different. It would be amazing. Many people live their lives blindly, just living, just being. So many people go to their graves settling, not exercising their right to have a blissful life. It's not their fault—they don't know any better—and this is part of understanding people, the way they were brought up, their environment, their past and present, and giving them permission to behave (for the most part) the way they do.

Society has trapped us into believing in the almighty dollar and instant gratification, and that medication will fix everything. It won't. Society has convinced us that it's okay to live in fear of the unknown. If you don't understand something, it's your responsibility to seek out the truth. YOUR truth. Everyone's truth can (and will) be different, and that is awesome.

Your life should be seen as a long-term commitment, not a short-term one. For anything you do, believe in your soul: "It's getting me to where I want to end up." Not getting something you desire now doesn't mean you won't get it later at a point where it makes more sense to have it. You still have lessons to learn along the way that you haven't learned yet.

There's always a divine appointment for everything. No timing is imperfect. That doesn't necessarily mean this book or what I'm describing will resonate with you right now, because on your journey of life, you may not be ready to receive what I'm talking about. And that's okay. It doesn't mean you're dumb; it means that from a spiritual level, you're not at a point that this makes sense. You have to be ready for soul setting, and the timing has to be on your terms, not others' terms. Relax.

Perspective

We all have a view of what reality is, and it's so different for everyone. It's crazy how perspective isn't merely how the world is seen differently through different eyes. Your reality is right for you, and my reality is right for me. Well then, which reality is wrong?

No reality is wrong. How can someone else's perspective be wrong for them when you aren't in their body? You haven't walked in their shoes or experienced what they've experienced.

There are vast numbers of people in the world who have a skewered perspective that forces them to sit in depression, anxiety, fear, worry, self-doubt, guilt, and a host of other maladies. They tend to live that way day after day, month after month, and for many people, year after year. Their version of life is skewered based on their individual circumstances. They are basing their lives on what's going on outside of their mind/ego, and it doesn't correspond with what they think should be going on, so they resist—and the struggle game begins.

We're not taught this as children because the vast majority of this world is aware that they shouldn't follow the outside world, but rather their inside world, for inner peace. It's ludicrous.

But I have great news! If this is you, I want you to pay attention to this chapter, because I believe soul setting will change your perspective. You aren't aware that there is another perspective because of your own reality.

CHAPTER 6 | 96

STORY TIME

I would love to become a professional golfer.

Do you have any idea what a golfer goes through to be on the PGA tour? Hours of practice. Hitting balls on a driving range. Hiring a coach. Driving and flying from one tournament to another, hoping you qualify.

It's not all that it's cracked up to be—we see only the pro tournaments on TV, and we don't see the amateur tournaments you have to endure. Then there's the weight room and the diet the golfer has to maintain.

They say that the game is eighty percent mental, and that's where I get hung up. Unfortunately, my temper can sometimes get the better of me. Aside from that, I love being outdoors, just walking the course and being one with nature (in my case with golfing, being one with the woods). On a good day, I can shoot around eighty, but the sky is the limit on a bad day. I've played some beautiful courses in my lifetime, and I don't even come close to eighty.

Here's the thing: If I had Tiger Woods himself coaching me, there isn't a chance in Hades that my capabilities would allow me to become a professional golfer on the PGA tour. "That's just negative thinking," you might say. No. It's reality, and if you're me, and if you're in tune with your natural, God-given talents, then you would realize that being a pro golfer just isn't in the cards for you. If you can do that, you'll go a long way in saving yourself from anguish and heartache.

I'm not trying to quash anyone's dreams here. Soul setting is based on reality, not delusion. People have spent years and years wasting their time on delusional wish-fulfillment to become things that they really aren't designed to be.

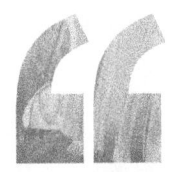

We suffer more on the inside than on the outside without realizing it.

/ Levy /

Faith and Struggle

This is the creed that I really live by, and it's deep within my soul: It's a life that creates possibilities. A life through faith can decrease depression and anxiety when practiced correctly. There is a higher power in my life.

This chapter isn't going to discuss God and religion. It is, however, going to be about someone or something looking after my best interests at all times. Sure, from time to time it might not seem like it, since there are situations and circumstances that happen frequently that we really don't prefer.

When we face a situation that isn't going our way, the human thing to do is to fight back and try to manipulate the outside world to match the world we see on the inside. This is called "struggling."

When our life isn't going the way we planned, we try to change the way things are going. We try to change people and what they're doing. This is called "resisting."

When the ego dies, the soul awakes...

/ Mahatma Gandhi /

Most of the time, this is futile.

Look at your current situation. Maybe your health is poor. Perhaps you don't have enough money. Maybe you have no job, you're about to be evicted from your home, your relationships with family and friends have become strained. These are circumstances that anyone can face. Sit down and ask yourself, "Can I change the circumstance that I'm in?" Most of the time, you can't. Through soul setting, you'll find that everything that's happening *to* you is exactly because; IT JUST IS. Remember things don't happen to you they happen *for* you.

Wait a minute! I said, "most of the time," right? Yes, I did, and sure, there are times when you have some control over what's going on. For example, perhaps you realized that, say, the argument you're having with your wife, brother, parents, or friend is a direct result of your outside view not matching your inside view. You realize that the other person has an environment or experience that you're not aware of that's leading them to have a completely different view. Understanding this can take you a long way. Maybe that's something that can help you begin to heal the relationship. Keep in mind that in most arguments, most of the drama you find yourself in was either created by you or contributed to by you.

The situation that you're in can be attributed to the decisions you've made in the past. These decisions were made with what you knew at the time. Take our parents, for example. Frequently, we look at the decisions our parents made, and we realize that they were poor decisions. Maybe they were, maybe they weren't. Either way, they were decisions made with what our parents knew through their own upbringing, their environment, and the way they perceived life and the future.

From time to time, doubt will creep in—and here we go, our mind takes over again.

Remember what our purpose in the world is? Let me remind you: either you will struggle, or you will grow spiritually. As you develop your self-awareness and your inner peace, your ego will drop by from time to time to let you know that it's still around. This is the same kind of problem we have when we diet, or when we try to change habits. We try to change our mindset and our ego says, "Not this time!" Frankly, it usually wins, and we revert to our old ways. This is due to fear, and the usually negative self-talk that devours what you're trying to accomplish. Soul setting to inner peace takes time and patience because the mind will fight you the whole way. Understanding this in advance will go a long way in your journey for a fulfilling life.

Whenever my life is in distress, I see it as an opportunity to find out why. Most of the time it's because I'm heading in the wrong direction. I realize that my higher power is telling me, "Nope, not that way!" If I'm not self-aware, if I'm not soul setting, I won't catch it—and that's exactly why so many people continue to live a life of struggle. They aren't listening to their soul. If something you perceive as bad, like losing your house, losing your job, losing your spouse to divorce—losing, losing, losing. In my view, any or all of these just means that there is something better coming.

And it usually does. How do I know? Because I've lived it, and so have you. You survive, and something always happens, because it must.

Dealing with Stress

I can't possibly go into detail about how to deal with stress in its entirety; however, I can give you a few suggestions.

HOW TO DEAL WITH STRESS

- Exercise regularly
- Eat well-balanced, nutritious meals
- Eliminate smoking and alcohol
- Deep breathing
- Develop patience and faith
- Take a break
- Make time for hobbies
- Talk about your problems
- Go easy on yourself
- Learn emotional intelligence

One of the main methods that I don't mention in the above list is exactly what we're discussing here: *Soul Setting*.

When you learn to accept things in the outside world

as they come (instead of resisting life), your struggles will diminish, and your stress will reduce dramatically. When your inside world doesn't match your outside world, this is where stress loves to hide and pop out over time. When stress occurs, your health can be compromised in the following ways:

- Prolonged periods of poor sleep
- Regular, severe headaches
- Unexplained weight gain or loss
- Feelings of isolation, withdrawal, or worthlessness
- Constant anger and irritability
- Loss of interest in activities
- Constant worrying or obsessive thinking
- Excessive alcohol or drug use
- Inability to concentrate

STORY TIME

> For over a decade, fighting with depression, anxiety, and stress played a huge role in my life. I didn't sleep well, I was often irritable and angry, and I didn't get a lot done. I can remember driving back two hours from court, because my ex-wife was again fighting me for more money and less access to my children. This went on for years and years. It was very stressful only because I didn't know about soul setting.
> I couldn't make my outside life match the way my inside life wanted. I didn't want her to bring me to

court again, but I didn't have any say in the matter, and I couldn't control what she did. I struggled and I didn't accept it, and this struggle occurred daily.

This particular day, driving home, I can remember saying to myself, "Boy, I can't wait to get home and have a drink." And that's exactly what I did. I got out of the car, opened the front door, and went straight to the kitchen cupboard and poured myself a drink. I can still taste the liquor, and feel the stress melt away. Man, that was what I needed. What a mind-control, abstract realization that was. In truth, the stress never melted away—it was only made worse.

Depression

Let's look at depression. Depression is a word we use to describe a persistent feeling of sadness and loss of interest. How do we know we're stuck in depression? The only way of knowing is that at some point in your life, you must have had a life that was satisfying, and happiness was part of that life. Everything in life has an opposite reaction: happy/sad, rich/poor, healthy/unhealthy. In order for you to feel some emotion, you first had to have felt the opposite emotion. This is called duality. So as possible as it is to be in a persistent state of sadness, the opposite must be true as well: a persistent feeling of happiness.

But what happens? The mind/ego comes into play here. The soul doesn't create this shift in your duality, the mind does. It usually occurs when self-doubt creeps in. It's a perspective we tell ourselves based on our history, experience, what we were told was the truth by our parents when we were children, and society.

How do you know if you're suffering from depression, or if you're in some kind of depressed state? It's only logical to assume that at one point, you were happy. This is the only way you can realize that you're depressed. Does it not make sense that if you feel depressed at any point, you have the ability to feel happy again? This has to be true, because if you say you're depressed, you have nothing to compare it to except happiness. And if you were in a state of happiness all the time and never entered the world of depression, then depression wouldn't exist—but it has to. This is equilibrium in the world.

When you think you are in a depressed state, it's important to try to obtain equilibrium. But how does one go about doing that? Here are some ideas:

Be reasonable. People have a limit to resources like time, money, and energy.

Find a support system.

Take control and say NO.

Make a schedule for rest.

Focus on today.

Depression is a way of letting you know that something is out of balance in your life, so pay attention. The human body is a miraculous network of nervous systems. Let's take a look at two in particular: The sympathetic and parasympathetic nervous systems.

The sympathetic nervous system is responsible for the

fight or flight response in your body. After the emergency situation passes, your body goes into a parasympathetic state, which is responsible for the body's recovery and relaxation mode. The parasympathetic nervous system is also responsible for the balance and order of this calm and restored state. When your body is constantly challenged by anxiety or worrying, the higher stress could cause detrimental effects to the digestive system as well as high blood pressure, the formation of artery-clogging deposits, and brain changes that may contribute to anxiety, depression, and addiction.

Living in a sympathetic mode can be detrimental to your overall health. Other side effects of living in this state include:

Fatigue

Headaches

Decreased immunity

Sleep problems

Mood swings

Sugar and caffeine cravings

Irritability or light-headedness between meals

Eating to relieve fatigue

Dizziness when moving from sitting or lying to standing

Digestive distress

Awareness of these stressors can help you in soul setting. The more you're aware of them, the faster you can respond to that stressor.

Of course, taking all of this into account, you do need to struggle in your life to grow. Remember, one of the two purposes in everyone's life is to grow spiritually, and in order to do this, we need to struggle. You want to struggle in your life to a degree. If you don't struggle, how do you improve, or obtain a better life? You won't—you'll just become stagnant. You won't reach your true potential. You have to be somewhat sympathetic towards people who live a life of relative ease. They can't grow. So, consider yourself blessed if you've been chosen to go through hell.

Thoughts versus Emotions

What is the worst disease known to humankind? It is a negative thought.

Your thoughts are not who you are. Your mind/ego creates millions of thoughts per day, some of which you don't even realize because they are unconscious. They're just thoughts. Think about this—you have a thought, and depending on your interpretation of it, you may be basing it on your past history of events and experiences, your values and morals, your upbringing, and other factors. Another person can have the exact same thought, but with different outcomes.

Let's use an example: You see someone eating an ice cream cone in the park, and because of that, you decide to have an ice cream cone yourself. Another person in the park sees the exact same person eating an ice cream cone and says, "Wow, how can they eat ice cream? That's disgusting!" There's no further action for this thought on the part of that person. It's crazy, I know. Everyone has thoughts, but it's the interpretation of those thoughts that determines what happens next.

Thoughts can be realistic or delusional. For a lot of people, their thoughts can be delusional, and they try to act on them, only to be disappointed in the end. Their thoughts play a huge role in this. Thoughts originate from the soul through energy from the outside world. These thoughts are discarded from others. For example, if someone else has a negative thought and they understand it is a negative thought, they can discard it to their outside world and that energy (thought) goes to the next person whose frequency is the same as theirs. If your frequency is the same as the person who discarded this (thought), it's up to you to determine whether those thoughts are realistic or not.

Your thoughts determine your experiences; therefore, you experience what you think. This is how emotions play a huge role in your thoughts. Again, your emotions aren't who you are, either. Your emotions only triggered the thought. You can't get angry without an interpretation of a thought. If you don't have thought, you can't have an emotion.

Another example: How can the thought of a snake be gentle to one person, and repulsive to someone else? Your experience with these creatures is how. One person's father raised snakes, so he doesn't have a fear of snakes. The other person was bitten by a snake as a child. Your thoughts can create your best life, or a life full of fear.

Thoughts play a huge part in the way you live and attract energy. If you think negative thoughts, then negative energy will be manifested. The contrary is also true: If you think positive thoughts, then you'll be surrounded by positive energy. Remember, these thoughts aren't you, even though we think they are. Thoughts are basically meaningless until we give them meaning through action or emotion. Negative thoughts can get us frustrated, and even angry. The only way a thought can get us angry is if we give it meaning and let emotion take us for a ride. Therefore, if we give the thought zero meaning and don't react to it, it will die. The next time a negative thought comes into your mind, and it brings a negative connotation, try to release it and let it go by replacing it with a positive thought. Give that negative thought zero reaction or emotion.

This is why I tend to subscribe to the belief that mind setting is dangerous. Thoughts don't come from the soul, they come from the mind. Here we are, in a day and age where we're trying to find inner peace, trying to free our mind, trying to stop the chatter in our minds. How can we when so many people are talking about mind setting: a positive mindset, a money mindset, etc.

It doesn't make sense to me to work on your mind when your mind is the issue. Working on your soul will allow the mind to be free because you're not thinking through your mind. When a thought comes up from your unconsciousness to your consciousness, evaluate it and see what energy you should give it. This can take time to learn, but it's worth it.

Perspective

Perspective is an opportunity to dig out of the hole you're in. If you open yourself up to possibilities that while negative energy can be powerful for you, positive energy can be exactly the same.

But how do we get there? That's the way you master your life. By understanding soul setting, you create a new identity for yourself in such a way that those low states will never return.

Is It Possible to Never Get into a State of Depression Again?

The power of the mind is critical in reaching a state of understanding and in transforming your identity to one of acceptance and not resistance. When you learn to accept most of what's going on outside your soul (instead of trying to control it), your inner life will be prepared to accept other positive energy with which you can work on your life—the way you want to create it, not force it. The benefits of acceptance in your life have many positive results: your health; your mental and emotional states improving drastically; all your relationships (partners, spouses, relatives, co-workers, and yes, even strangers you meet); and with the help of financial literacy, your net worth position can also change dramatically.

How many times have you been cut off in traffic, or burnt your toast, or someone at work did something you didn't like, or you've gotten a flat tire—the list goes on. Could you control most of those situations? More than likely, no. Still, the person who cut you off may not have seen you, or was in a hurry, or had one of any number of valid reasons for doing what they did.

Every morning you do what you normally do for years, and that is use the same toaster to make toast for breakfast.

You put the bread in and push down the button, but for some reason the button malfunctions, and it stays longer in the down position than normal, causing your bread to burn. Did you know in advance that the toaster was going to malfunction? No, of course not. Is that something you wanted to happen—have burnt toast this morning? Of course not. Is there anything you could have done to prevent this? Again, the answer is no. Accepting it and moving on is therefore the best alternative for a stress-free morning.

You would do well to Google Peter Crone, as he has a quote that can help ease your life: "Life will present you with people and circumstances to reveal where you're not free."

That last scenario, if I'm to be truly honest with you, drives me nuts. I usually can get very upset about this, as I wanted my toast for breakfast. And there it is! My circumstance where I'm not free. Not being able to control my emotions and most of the stuff that truly won't matter in one, two, or five years. Seriously, Levy, you're going to get angry over something you can't control, like a broken toaster?

Your mind works against yourself every day. Your soul works for you, not against you. You have paid an enormous price to listen to your mind, and that price is your freedom. You are a prisoner, and you are found guilty of crimes against yourself. There are other perspectives in life. This is the power. Learn other perspectives, because currently you know only one perspective, and that is YOURS. The only issue you have is that life isn't going the way you want it or expect it to. You can't engineer your outside world. It's going to do whatever it's going to do, with or without your input, because it doesn't need your input.

> **You don't have to worry, because what will be, will come.**
>
> / Levy /

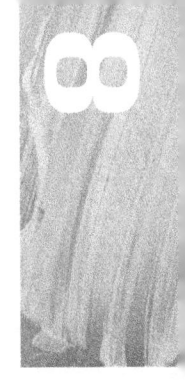

Stress

Stress and How It Affects Us

Understanding your own pain through a traumatic event as a child can give you some perspective on other people's behavior. Many people have not accepted what has happened to them and continue to resist, and therefore, the struggle continues. This struggle shows up in every aspect of their lives. What can happen when you struggle with your past without accepting it? Your health can suffer. Psychologically, we continue to struggle in our minds, which can translate into physiological issues like high blood pressure, altered hormonal balances and sleep cycles, weakened immune systems, addiction issues, decreased libido, and increased weight.

What happened, happened, and it couldn't have happened any other way ... because it didn't.

/ Peter Crone /

STORY TIME

As recently as just a few years ago, any little thing would set me off. Most of the time, it was things in my mind/ego that weren't working out the way I thought they should have, or things that were taking too long, or mistakes I made that I shouldn't have made. *Does this sound familiar?* Take a look at yourself. Did the waitress bring you the wrong coffee? Was the elevator out of order, and you had to walk up a few flights? Did a car cut you off this morning on the way to the office? Did you miss your bus? The list could go on and on. I can remember that the cafeteria where I used to work had a menu that showed the weekly meals. Wednesday was always macaroni and cheese day. One of my favorites, and it made Monday and Tuesday awesome, because I couldn't wait until Wednesday.

Well, once Wednesday came, and I didn't see any macaroni and cheese on the trays. "No mac and cheese today?" I asked one of the ladies who was serving.

"No, I'm sorry, we had a problem with stock," she replied.

Man, I lit up on her. "Your menu said mac and cheese today," I said.

When she looked at me, you could almost read her facial expression: What the heck is his problem?

It's only mac and cheese. "We have pork chops," she said weakly.

Naturally, I muttered an F-bomb, and said, "Fine, give me the pork chop."

As I tell you this story, all I can think about was what a jerk I was. It wasn't her fault; after all, she wasn't in charge of ordering the food. Still, this is a good example of my outside world not matching my inside world, which created a conflict.

I had two options here: first, I could resist and get upset, which put me in struggling mode, and the energy that I put out was negative, which means I'd attract more negative energy, causing the afternoon to go poorly. Or, Option Two: I could just accept the change in menu and move on, as I had no control over it. Once you accept this option into your soul, you let it go, never to have it bother you again.

How do you know it's in your soul? This, to me, is the easy part. You know it's in your soul because you really don't get mad about it. Your day isn't affected by it whatsoever. If you think you have it in your soul and you get upset, or it still affects you after it's happened, then it's not in your soul, it's still in your mind/ego.

As you look at the macaroni and cheese incident, you can see where I fit into it. I was overreacting. You might be thinking to yourself, *I would never overreact to this situation.* However, I'm betting that you've overreacted to things many times that I may not have. We're all humans.

My reaction to the outside world not

corresponding to my inside world is totally different now. Still, it's a process. For the most part, I'm still growing in this department.

MUST READ!

Let's talk about what stress does—and this pertains to most of the stress that we cause ourselves unnecessarily. When you feel stress, your body releases a bunch of hormones. One hormone in particular, cortisol, is nicknamed "the stress hormone." This hormone under stress conditions decreases your IQ by about fifty percent within around eight minutes. Excess cortisol is dangerous because it's basically poison. If your body experiences chronic stress, you begin to feel unpleasant side effects, such as:

- Fatigue
- Irritability
- Headaches
- Intestinal problems, such as constipation, bloating, or diarrhea.
- Anxiety or depression
- Weight gain
- Increased blood pressure
- Low libido, erectile disfunction, or problems with regular ovulation or menstrual periods.
- Difficulty recovering from exercise.
- Poor sleep.

None of this happens overnight. This can take years to develop, however, as with eating doughnuts, you won't notice the weight gain overnight. It can take months or even years to notice. If you don't know how to manage stress, the effects can be deadly.

A life of constant, daily stress can result in:

- Increased blood sugar levels
- Weight gain
- A suppressed immune system
- Digestive problems
- Heart disease

Indicators that you may be under too much stress include:

- Am I taking on too much? Do I need help?
- Am I overreacting?
- Am I trying to do things too perfectly?
- Am I expecting too much from others?
- Do I need to say "no" more often?

STORY TIME

Let's use me as an example. I had a lot of stress due to my not accepting the outside world for what it was: a world I have very limited control over (if any at all). I often shifted into anger mode, which affected some of my relationships—and not in a good way. I never hit anyone, I would just get very upset, and the occasional golf club would mysteriously fly out of my hand on the course. Similarly, on the job site, the occasional hammer would leave my hand. The "F-Bombs" would fly free. During my ten years of court battles with my ex, I developed into a full-on alcoholic. I'm not blaming her—I was doing the best I could with what I knew at the time. My stress drove me to seek out stress relievers, and alcohol filled that void. The stress never went away completely, but when I was drinking, it seemed to disappear.

    This method proved to be desperately futile. It didn't solve anything except to create a different identity for me. I wasn't the same person. You see, when you drink, the neurotransmitters that control your thinking process can be affected, and in my case, it was. Sleepless nights developed, and depression and anxiety soon followed. I was falling apart.

    With the help of my family (and after a few issues with the law), I decided to quit drinking. Over time, my thinking process began to shift. I've been sober for around nineteen years as I write this book, and I've really noticed my thinking process is much different than it used to be. I've been able to analyze myself to try to figure out why this stress, this depression, this anxiety, was plaguing me. I began to examine why my life wasn't going the way I wanted it to.

    It was during this time (about twenty-plus years) that I discovered "soul setting." I began to understand the past and how it affects each and every one of us. I began to understand how past decisions based on our experiences, environments, and how we were raised played an integral part of our identities.

The Physical Body: Psychological versus Physiological

Understanding that there is a direct correlation between your soul and your physical body will give you an advantage over others. Psychological means the mental or emotional state of the mind. When you suffer from depression and anxiety, it isn't the soul that creates this issue, it's the mind. Once again, the mind/ego is a root cause for many issues that you will suffer with physiologically. Why not take the ego out of the equation and think with your soul?

What is physiology? Physiology is the study of the human body, which is a branch of biology that deals with the functions of life and living matter (such as organs, tissues, or cells) and of the physical and chemical phenomenon involved. Physiology is the study of the body, and psychology is the study of the mind. The two interact with one another.

Let's look at an example of how they do this. You're late for a meeting and you hit a traffic jam. What happens? Your mind creates emotions like anxiety. This is psychological stress that is a catalyst for physiological stress and physical changes in your nervous system. This is where the fight-or-flight instincts come into play. This creates stress in the body.

Now the body goes to work to deal with this stress. The brain sends a message to the nervous system, which then releases cortisol. The heart beats faster, and blood rushes more quickly through your body. Can you imagine this happening over and over during the course of your lifetime? The poor heart doesn't even have a chance because it's working so hard all the time.

This is just a small sample of the cumulative effect that stress has on your body. Not being able to handle stress properly can cause severe damage to your body. Stress affects your respiratory, digestive, and muscular systems as well. Your lungs breathe more rapidly. Your liver produces extra glucose for energy. Your muscles tense up to protect themselves.

If all this sounds exhausting to you, you're right. And when the stress doesn't go away because of your high-stress job or your constant, on-the-go lifestyle, your body can't keep up.

Addiction and the Mind

I'm not a doctor. But what I do have is more than fifty years of life experience and thirty-five years of research on how to become successful in life. Most of that research was for my own financial reasons: I have always wanted to be a millionaire, and I started my quest early. I did a lot of research and was in more MLM (multi-level marketing) plans that I can count. I've spent thousands of dollars on these schemes only to make very little money—as a matter of fact, I've spent more money to get into them than I've made in return. Rule number one: If you have to pay to get a job or into a company, that should be a red flag. Don't do it.

Now that I've been clean and sober for more than eighteen years, my mind works differently. My decision-making process is clearer and more precise.

If your life isn't on the right track, take a long, hard look at your recreational activities. Do they include drugs or alcohol? If they do, can you be objective and realistic about them? Can you conclude that they are blunting the mental edge you need to think clearly about your future, and what you want out of life? If you can't be objective with yourself, then I suggest talking to family and friends and asking them to be candid. Ask them if they think that you have a drinking issue, or if you smoke too much weed. See what kind of answer they give you.

Soul setting is the ability to stop thinking with your mind and start thinking with your soul. It's understanding that life happens. IT JUST IS. It's having faith that the future will look after you. The future will happen whether you do something or not. When you adopt this lifestyle, your energy changes, and you start to have inner peace. You will accept life as it happens, and you'll be okay with it, because you have to be. If you don't like life as it's happening, look at what you can control, which is usually your inner self. As you enter self-awareness (or spiritual awareness), you will enter a freedom that you've never felt before.

The reason I drank so much is that it was a coping mechanism. It was how I dealt with stress. Now that the stress is gone, I have no use for alcohol, because I don't have to COPE with life anymore. I just live it.

From the depths of my soul, I can tell you that the best thing I ever did was to quit drinking. And the funny thing is that the worst days of my life turned out to be the best part of my life. It was an opportunity for me to change directions. I know for a fact that my higher power was calling me and looking out for me, even though I couldn't see it at the time.

Why do so many people go to their graves stressed?

This world of ours isn't complex, but we make it so through instant gratification. If we lived for our true purpose (which is to help one another and to grow spiritually), our lives would have much, much more meaning, and you would see a huge, profound change in yours.

There are seven avenues I believe you really need to master and nurture in order to have inner peace:

The relationship between patience, time, and energy.
Understanding others.
Struggle and sacrifice.
Reality versus delusion.
The physical body.
Emotional intelligence.
Financial intelligence.

Notice that financial intelligence is last. Yes, money is important; however, without mastering the first six avenues, your ability to accumulate wealth will be very difficult (which is the reason so many people in the world have issues financially).

Why Aren't People Happy?

hap·py
/ˈhapē/
adjective
feeling or showing pleasure or contentment.
"Melissa came in looking happy and excited."

Notice the word *contentment* is in the definition.

con·tent·ment
/kənˈtentmənt/
noun
a state of happiness and satisfaction

You can't always be happy. If it weren't for sadness, you wouldn't know what happiness is. Ying and yang, right?

Many people spend their lives chasing happiness. You should never chase anything: not relationships, not money, and especially not happiness. The more we pursue something, the further away from us it tends to get. When someone or something is meant to be with you, the world will help you obtain it (again, *if* it's meant to be with you).

Try obtaining contentment. I'm not telling you to *settle*. When soul setting is correctly in place, you learn that life is going to happen for you whether you do something or not. It is in the action that life occurs and the reaction you have with it.

Your needs and wants revolve around this so-called "happiness." When you don't get what you want, then depression and anxiety tend to creep in, right? That's because you're chasing happiness. Life isn't designed for you to chase happiness. How do I know? How are you feeling right now with your life? This is the whole purpose of this book, to try to show that your soul will help you obtain the difference between needs and wants. You have everything you require on the inside to obtain your desire on the outside. Everyone does. Concentrate on the inside.

Settling and contentment are two very different things. Settling is doing nothing. Remember the definition of "happy" above: Happy is an emotion, and emotions are temporary. We want something for our lives that is more permanent.

Contentment is a state of happiness. Contentment requires action, not sitting there and doing nothing. When you are content with life *as it is*, realizing the outside world is going to occur as it does. But when your soul setting is in its place, then your inside will have many happy moments.

So how will you know that you're content with the outside world?

When you're struggling with life, you know it. When you're depressed or filled with anxiety, you feel it. When you accept life on its terms and not yours, then you will feel it in your soul, and none of those other feelings will come up. When you're working towards a life you want, then you will no longer have to put pressure on yourself. Yes, of course, you'll need to work hard and take action, but with that action comes results, and those results are what you should be content with. If you take no action and do very little, those results will also show, and you most likely will become depressed. Your mind will get in the way, and your soul will not be set.

When you think with your soul and you're working but the results are not what you want, then one of two things may be happening: You're thinking with your mind about what you want, and you're on the wrong path. Depression and anxiety will often tell you that.

You're still chasing something.

True contentment doesn't come from the outer world. When you're acting towards your realistic life, it seems natural, and you look forward to waking up each day with the faith that your life is exactly where it is. Accepting life on its terms and not yours and having soul setting faith will create a life you desire. You will be aligned with the world.

Purpose and Passion

This is one of my favorite topics, because during my journey, it came up so frequently—and it created nothing by depression and anxiety.

Gurus tell you not to quit on your dreams, so you don't, and you get nowhere. Why? Generally speaking, when you define your purpose and your passion, you aren't listening to your soul (which is inside of you). You are instead listening and looking to what's outside of you. You look around and see what others have. Let's face it, this is a materialistic world, and while I'm not saying there's anything wrong with things per se, but when you focus on them and spend your money on them when you can't afford them, depression tends to set in. I may want the Rolex, the fine cars, and the beautiful vacation houses . . . but I'm also aware that these things won't make me happy.

When your focus is on your goals, years can go by without achieving what you want, and here's why: You're focused on the end product, for example, the Rolex. You know it's going to cost you thousands of dollars to purchase, so you set out to save money and buy one. Unfortunately, life occurs, and you just can't save enough for that object of desire, creating only anxiety and depression. Most millionaires and billionaires are able to purchase their watches, cars, jewelry, vacations, etc., because they *invest*, not save. They invest their money in assets that *create* an income (rental properties, other businesses, stocks with dividends). This takes faith, consistency, patience, and financial literacy.

So, what is your purpose? Believe it or not, *everyone's* purpose is the same: to grow spiritually and help one another. That's it. And by spiritually, I don't mean religiously. Spiritually means internal growth (hence, soul setting). It means living a life that's quiet on the inside, with peace and freedom of the mind. This is where struggle occurs for many people. Wouldn't it be great if, say, ninety percent of your stress was gone? Keep reading this book, and I'll show you how I'm reaching this goal.

What is passion?
pas * sion
/ˈpaSHən/
noun
Strong and barely controllable emotion

"a man of impetuous passion"
The suffering and death of Jesus
"meditations on the Passion of Christ"

When you Google the word "passion," this is what you might find. Notice the words "suffering" and "Jesus" are in the sentence (just saying). For so many people, passion tends to have a financial component in terms of what you have to be, or should be, passionate about. We look for either fame, or fortune, or something with a "wow" factor to it.

This couldn't be farther from the truth of what passion is. Passion is simply something you love to do. When you are doing what you love, time simply flies by.

How to Find Your Passion

This is the crux of the issue. We might be told, "You are looking for a passion when a passion finds you." This is a misconception about passion. Passion has and always will be inside you.

Let's use me as an example. In sixth grade, my best friend Rob and I were in class together, and we would doodle on paper. At that time, we thought we would end up living together and marrying girls at some point and each of us having a family, all while traveling together in an eighteen-wheeler (what were we thinking?). We started to design the back of the trailer to accommodate our families. This included a kitchen, living room, two bedrooms, and a bathroom. We didn't have a clue how the electrical would work, and we seriously thought the toilet would be a hole in the floor, through which we could do our business on the highway as we sped along at a hundred miles per hour. We designed so many trailers and so many scenarios, and we loved doing it.

Fast forward to what I love doing today: designing houses and buildings. That's what I've been doing for the last twenty years. We purchase houses and change their entire layouts, from redesigning the kitchens to building additions. We were flipping houses and teaching the Property Brothers a thing or two before it became huge. I was self-taught, no schooling, and loved it. Today, I still dabble in real estate.

When I started, I never thought about the money. I always wanted to be wealthy, but I didn't know this was the route I'd be going on. I ended up purchasing a duplex, living in one half while renting out the other, refinancing, and then purchasing another one. Once I started, I really loved renovations, especially the design aspect. I would easily spend twelve hours a day doing this, and I was excited to wake up the next morning at six and do it all over again.

My point about money is this: forget about it for a moment and pretend you didn't have to worry about it. What would you do with your time? What do you do that you get lost in while you're doing it? What did you think about doing when you were twelve years old? Listen to your soul without thinking about what will bring fame or fortune. After all, I know people who are millionaires who love what they do but only make a modest amount of money doing it. It's not what they did for a living that created this wealth, but how they invested their money. They did what they loved first and foremost.

> **You as you know yourself is not the end of you.**
>
> / Levy /

Trauma

Is There Such a Thing as "Trauma"?

Are you the victim of circumstances or a victim of your own conditioning? Are you a victim of programming during your younger years? Now it's your turn to decode your programming so that you can evolve.

We can't really define trauma, because so many people have different variations or degrees of their own trauma. Let's look at some examples.

**Trauma isn't what happens to you,
it's what happens inside you.**

/ Gabor Mate /

WARNING: The examples I'm about to use are graphic, but as real as anyone might be able to imagine.

- Growing up in a war-torn region, in which you watch militants assassinate your father before your eyes.
- Living in a war-torn region, where a bomb goes off, killing members of your family, and you have to flee to an unknown and unfamiliar area.
- You're a front-line worker (such as a police officer, firefighter, or paramedic), and you witness the bloody aftermaths of numerous accidents.
- You're a member of a trauma unit at a hospital.
- A person you trusted (or maybe you didn't even know) molested you as a young person.
- A loved one dies.
- You are the victim of a physical assault.
- You witness an event such as a stabbing or a shooting.
- You're a sixteen-year-old girl dating a boy for three years, and he cheats on you and breaks off the relationship.
- You get a failing grade, and your drunk father goes into a rage.

Part of the issue I have with the word "trauma" is that it can be overused or used incorrectly. We live in a world in which the concept of "trauma" has taken over our lives to mean any situation that we haven't processed logically. "Trauma" for far too many of us is the actual event that's taken place. That isn't the "trauma." The "trauma" is the feeling inside that it creates, not the actual event. It's how we process it—or fail to process it. The pain YOU create inside is much worse than the actual situation. It's the years of what's happened to you inside, and it grows because you give birth to fear, shame, or guilt. Please keep in mind that I don't take the term "trauma" lightly, nor do I make light of these situations. But I feel that in many cases (including mine), the term "trauma" was used, and I was brought into it and as a result, suffered for many years.

Let's use a specific example of "trauma." A little boy comes home with a failing grade. He has to get his parents to sign the report card. Unfortunately, the father has a drinking problem because he's dealing with his own depression. He goes into a rage and perhaps hits the boy—or, barring that, he screams and yells at the child, throwing objects around the room and slamming doors. The boy develops shame and guilt and fear over what's happened. Going forward, he now assumes deep in his mind that if he makes a mistake, people might go into a rage with him.

Incidents like these can snowball over time in our minds. The very thought of failing can cripple this hypothetical little boy, stopping him from ever trying something new. The thought grows in his mind. It multiplies. Up to now, the boy has been trying to cope with it. For the next five, ten, twenty years, that boy doesn't sit down and examine that situation for what it was: one drunk person unpacking his own baggage. He hasn't been able to look logically at that moment for what it was: something beyond his control.

"Trauma" usually camouflages the true reality of how

great our lives can be. Our lives have been distorted by a perspective that paints a picture of fear of the world. Sometimes, you don't realize it was the trauma that created this. Only through someone changing your perspective of the world can you create a logical understanding that this trauma was just that: one event, one person, compounded over the years by your mind/ego. Self-awareness is the key to unlocking your "trauma."

STORY TIME

I'd like to take a chapter out of my own life to illustrate how, after looking through different lenses of logic, I came to realize that what I went through was not trauma.

As you're aware by now, when I was twenty-six, and my marriage came to an end. We had a three-year-old girl and a one-year-old boy, and my children were my life. My ex decided that she wanted to date women. She took our children and moved two hours away. At the time, I was devastated, and I started drinking more than I usually did, going into a massive depression and planning my own suicide. Life couldn't have been at its lowest point for me, and I wanted out.

Within about two to three days of going through with my plan, a friend of mine beat me to it, leaving his twelve-year-old boy. That, by the grace of God, is what saved me.

For the next ten years, I descended into a pity party, and I sought help through a professional psychiatrist who gave me heavy medication, which really helped at the time. After a couple of years, the medication was turning my life into a blur, and realization began kicking in. I was still massively depressed, I lost my job, had no money, and was drinking like crazy. Moreso, I could see things weren't going to get better, as my mind/ego simply reinforced the idea that women were cruel. I didn't have to look very far for examples of this. I couldn't see that there were great women out there because I was focusing on how crappy my life was, and the so-called cruelty of women was just being illogically programmed into my mind.

Finally, after ten years, it all came to a halt when I spent a night in jail. My family followed up with an intervention, and eventually, I began crawling out of my hole. I went on to the thirty-day, in-house rehab center, and I haven't looked back since.

Today, as I look back twenty years later (clean and happily remarried), I realize what doctors had labeled as "trauma" wasn't trauma. It was simply and event that took place in my life that I didn't process properly.

I've mentioned this before, but I'll mention it again. If you're coping with your depression or anxiety by self-medicating through pills, alcohol, recreational drugs, or hard drugs, then it will be next to impossible to get freedom in your mind. These outside stimuli result in creating a different brain chemistry that will encourage and perpetuate your suffering. I know that after nearly twenty years, my thinking is now so much different than it was during my drinking days.

Responsibility For Your Life

Are you seriously going to blame your parents, the government, the market, etc., for your current situation? Here's an interesting thought to ponder: The common belief is that you're in charge of your own life. I have news for you—no, you aren't, you are in control only to a point. If you believe in a higher power, then that power is in control. To a degree, you're responsible for your situation. Your situation may be based on decisions made three to five years ago that are just showing up now. You have two choices to see how life unfolds for you. Life is good, or life is bad, and you and only you are responsible for this choice.

Most people are going down the wrong road and following a financial desire, goal, or dream. If you're doing so, it's not your fault—your responsibility is to be aware of this factor in our society. Society has created this through history of peasants, kings, and queens. Success tends to draw the scales towards the financial side. Society measures success through financial wealth and net worth. The person with the most toys, the biggest houses, the shiniest cars, wins.

This ridiculous notion has brought with it huge mental issues. These mental issues have become so huge that in this modern world, many people will suffer with some kind of mental issue. And that means struggling in one sense or another.

This is where soul setting comes into play. When I adopted this concept, my depression and anxiety totally disappeared. I no longer suffer, but I accept. I don't accept this mental issue; I accept the outside world as it is and as it comes. Understanding people and how they've developed as flawed human beings, I can now empathetically see where everyone has been. Now, the issue is whether everyone can understand everyone else, and figure out why they react the way they do.

As far as responsibility goes, we as individuals can no longer blame our history, and in some cases, our traumatic childhoods, for our current situations. We have two choices: Live in the present or live in the past as a victim. If you live as a victim, the negative energy that revolves around you will constantly be there, disempowering you as you continue your struggle in life.

The other choice you have is to accept your past and let go. I'm not saying that what happened to you was fair, right, your fault, or anything you deserve. However, it happened, and there's nothing you can do about the past. IT JUST IS. This acceptance that I refer to is merely the acceptance that the trauma occurred. It's not the acceptance that it was okay. But accepting the situation gives you the power of positivity, and you're able to move forward without struggling because you're accepting it for what it is: an event in the journey of your life. Use this event to help others strengthen you and grow spiritually so that you'll have inner peace.

> **The fastest way to change your life
> is to stop controlling your life.**
>
> / Levy /

Luck

Good Luck or Bad Luck: Is There Such a Thing?

I'm not a person who believes in luck. I'm also not a person who believes that people are in "the right place at the right time" or "the wrong place at the wrong time." These people are just there. That's it. IT JUST IS.

Have you ever heard the expression, "You are the prisoner of your own mind"? I really think Shakespeare said it best: "There is neither good nor bad, but thinking makes it so." Read that two or three times and sit with it. What does it mean to you? To me, it means that once again, the mind/ego will win either way. If you rely on luck, you're relying on your mind. If you think something happened that was bad, again, it wasn't bad until your mind crept in.

There is no such thing as good luck or bad luck, just God's blessings and lessons.

/ Unknown /

Let's listen to Franklin D. Roosevelt, who said, "I think we consider too much the good luck of the early bird and not enough of the bad luck of the early worm." Luck is perspective. It's how we look at circumstances and situations. Why do we need perspective? Why do we need to believe in luck at all? If we have zero preference (which I understand is difficult in some circumstances), then luck will not play a role in your life. Accept life AS IT IS.

One of the best fables I know comes from China: Many years ago, there was a wise peasant. He had a son who was the apple of his eye. The peasant was also the owner of a fine white stallion, which everyone admired. One day, his horse escaped from the grounds and disappeared. The villagers came to him one by one and said, "You're such an unlucky man. It's such bad luck that your horse escaped."

The peasant responded, "Who knows? Maybe it's bad, maybe it's good."

The next day, the stallion returned, followed by twelve wild horses. The neighbors visited him again and congratulated him on his luck. Again, he just said, "Who knows? Maybe it's good, maybe it's bad."

The next day, his son was attempting to train one of the wild horses when he fell and broke his leg. Once more, everyone came with their condolences: "It's terrible."

Again, he replied, "Who knows? Maybe it's good, maybe it's bad."

A few days passed, and his poor son was limping around the village with a broken leg. Then, the emperor's army entered the village, announcing that a war was starting, and they were enrolling all the young men in the village. However, they left the peasant's son since he had a broken leg. Everyone was extremely jealous of the peasant. They talked about his sheer luck.

Still, the old man just muttered, "Who knows? Maybe it's good, maybe it's bad."

If luck is perception, then one would think people would dictate their behavior accordingly: "I am such an unlucky person." This negative thought could be perceived as creating negative energy, which would attract negative situations. If that's true, then, the opposite must also be true: "I am the luckiest person in the world." This is a positive thought, so it should attract positive energy and a positive situation.

Thinking that luck can control your life can be somewhat dangerous. To rely on luck means you're relying on thought again. At this point, we're entering the realm of the mind, and you know what that means: some sort of mindset that has to be created again from scratch. A different mindset, and . . . man this is exhausting! If your soul setting is in place correctly, every event that occurs happens *for* you, and not *against* you. Remember that luck is just what we believe it to be: a random act.

> **My bad days are better than the average person's good days.**

/ Levy /

How to Start Your Journey

Awareness and patience. Being aware of the now, and not the past or the future, because neither one you can do anything about.

When you make decisions, what drives your decision-making process? Is it your mind or your soul? If you're thinking about a decision from, say, an economical position, you're probably being driven by your ego, and that isn't good. If you're thinking about a decision based on "What's in it for me?" you're again probably headed in the wrong direction. If you're aware and patient, your soul will let you know.

Faith is another word that resonates with me. For me, my creator, God, runs my show, not me. For you, if your creator is a law of attraction, energy, Budda, or whatever else it

---

**The soul always knows what to do to heal itself.
The challenge is to silence the mind.**

/ Caroline Myss /

may be, faith deep in your soul will go a long way in assisting your decision-making. You don't have to fully understand your direction and why you're going there, you just have to trust faith.

Faith

Make no mistake, this is a very difficult way of life to live if you've never done it before. As you get into soul setting and you work on changing your identity, this "no-preference" lifestyle will come to you. And I must admit that I still don't have it all worked out in this department. After all, I'm human, and I do have preferences—for the color of my truck, for example.

I was looking for a used truck for my business, one for the guys to use. My company's trucks are black, and they're Ford F-150s, so I'd like to maintain consistency when it comes to branding. I was looking for a black truck and found it nearly impossible to find. Once I decided I was okay with a white or gray or blue one, a black one appeared. How did I know I had this bit of soul setting correct when it came to a preference (or lack of one) for the color? I really meant it in my soul, and I wasn't just saying it in my mind/ego. I was looking at a couple of white trucks when a black truck came along. I didn't get upset when a white truck became available. I was patient. Remember, this is how you can tell whether you have soul setting in place correctly: You will not be disappointed. If you get upset that you didn't find a black truck, that means you had more of a preference than you thought, and it wasn't in your soul, it was still in your mind.

Keep in mind that a black truck or an apartment may not

appear right away (or at all) because it wasn't meant to be, or the timing wasn't correct for you. This is just a test to make sure your soul setting was correct. You accept the outside world for what it is: A world you cannot control. IT JUST IS.

My higher power (God) didn't create me and say, "Good luck, son, this world isn't very nice, and you will struggle all of your life." Or, if this isn't your higher power, your higher power didn't say to you as you entered the world, "This is going to be a terrible world for you but do the best you can." On the contrary. My higher power said, "There is abundance for everyone, not just for you, and in order to obtain your share of abundance, you must learn inner peace, and follow your soul, not your mind/ego."

I said before that I wasn't going to give a sermon, but here's a short one. Right in the Bible, it states in Romans 12:2, "Do not conform to the pattern of the world but be transformed by the renewing of your mind. Then you will be able to test and approve what God's will is—his good, pleasing, and perfect will." If we Google "What does being transformed by the renewing of your mind mean?" it will say: Meaning. Are you living your best life? Shifting your patterns and focus can change your life. That is what this verse is about: renewing your mind, changing the way you think, creating a better life for yourself, and a life that honors God. The world and society have patterns, or ways, that lead to a broken life. The way you change the way you think is through your soul. Your mind will automatically renew and give way to creativity. There is NOTHING you need to do with your mind.

Drama

Do you like drama? I didn't think so. I have a saying: "Most of the drama in your life is either created by you or contributed to by you." And most of that drama doesn't matter in the greater scheme of life. Are you upset that a coworker at the water cooler is always talking about how great they are or how wonderful their child is? Is a family member constantly making wrong decisions in his or her life, and you just don't approve? Is your neighbor talking behind your back and spreading rumors about you? Feeding into these will only contribute to your stress.

Learning how to let go of things that won't matter in six months will do a world of good. But, you say, "my daughter is dating a total jerk," or, "my neighbor said something that's affecting my friendship with another neighbor," or, "my wife comes up with crazy ideas that drive me nuts." These are all examples of everyday life. We all come from different environments, and we're raised differently with different morals and values, and those experiences create who we are. Understanding that and having empathy for others will serve you well.

Let's face it, none of us are perfect. Your daughter will have to go through her experience to realize that maybe her boyfriend is a jerk, but that's on her. You could express your feelings respectfully and ask her where she thinks her relationship is going, but you'll probably get backlash from her. Expect it and move on. You've said your piece. Maybe the validity of what the neighbor said to the other neighbor about you is up to the neighbor who heard the rumor. If that puts a strain on your relationship, what kind of friend is that person when he or she didn't respect you enough to come up to you and ask you about it? Do you really need fake friends who believe in rumors? And when it comes to your wife, you know that she comes up with crazy ideas from time to time. Has she ever followed through on any of them? Chances are that she hasn't. If she does, and she doesn't hurt anyone including herself, is there any harm in her continuing?

These circumstances are on you, not the other person. Your knee-jerk reaction to defend yourself and criticize others will only create negative energy, so let it go. By being self-aware of your emotions and quickly analyzing whether they serve you or not, and learning to let go quickly and move on, will eventually become your new standard of behavior, instead of lashing out quickly with emotional reactions.

Increased Faith for the Future

As I've mentioned, I'm a Christian, so my higher power is God. This book isn't meant to convert anyone, but whatever your higher power is, I really tend to lean into mine. If you understand and practice soul setting daily (and even hourly), when it comes to decisions on how to react to different situations and individuals, you'll see that your faith in a bright future ahead of you will increase steadily. Your present may not always seem bright, but you can accept what is going on around you, and that your higher power always has your back.

Let's take a look at an example from your own life. You may be going through something right now, and if you aren't, that's awesome. In that case, try to think of a time in your life that was difficult. Some of you may be constantly bringing that time forward into your life today. If you are, then that's struggling, and you're most likely resisting it. If you got through the tough time, try to remember the time when it wasn't fun. When we look at that situation now, you can probably see how things might have gotten better for you since then, or at least aligned you for the better.

STORY TIME

I'll use my life as an example. When my ex-wife decided she wanted a divorce, it was devastating, so much so that I wanted to end my life. I was planning it, and something else happened to me, a friend of mine beat me to it, leaving behind a son. Fast-forward ten years, and I was still struggling. Why? I was resenting my ex-wife for what she had done to me and my children. Could I control what she was doing? No.

When I fell into the discovery of soul setting, I decided to stop resisting what was happening and take full responsibility for the divorce. I stopped resenting her and felt bad for her. I accepted everything she was doing (even though I didn't agree with it) and accepted that there was nothing I could do about her involvement in the situation. All I could do was deal with how I reacted to her.

Boy, did my life change! The negative energy left and was replaced by renewed faith. Over the next ten to fifteen years of my life, I fell in love with a woman whom I met after my divorce, but whom I initially wouldn't give the time of day. She wasn't my type, I thought. It was Sharon, the mother of a friend of my son. After fifteen years of being with her as a friend, I decided to pop the question, and we've been content with many, many happy moments. If that divorce didn't happen, I wouldn't be writing this book, or even diving into how to live through soul setting.

My faith has increased daily, and I do mean daily. People irritate me from time to time, but I just empathize with them now. I feel compassion for them. For the most part, they just don't know any better. But faith now lives deep in my soul. I truly understand that my higher power is *always* looking out for me.

A comfortable mind is a dangerous mind.

/ Levy /

Patience, Time, and Energy

Emotional Intelligence

I would love to tell you the secret of life, but there isn't one. Anyone who tells you the word "secret," just run from them, as fast as you can. This is just a marketing term people love to use to get you excited enough to buy the secret to creating a million dollars in less than six months, or the secret to losing twenty-five pounds in three weeks—or how about this one: the secret to success or happiness. And the list goes on.

THERE ARE NO SECRETS. Think about it. A video comes out and it claims to have the secret to weight loss, and you watch it, and you notice that there are one million views. How much of a secret can it be? PLEASE don't get suckered into marketing ploys.

**In a very real sense, we have two minds:
one that thinks and one that feels.**

/ Daniel Goleman /

But I digress. Let's talk about Emotional Intelligence. This, to me, is the key (but not the secret) to living life free of stress and drama. Most of life is how we deal with everyday mundane situations and circumstances.

For example: a coworker talks to you about something you don't care about, a stranger cuts you off on the road, your children are making unreasonable demands, or the weather (yes, the weather!) is terrible. How do you deal will all this stuff? Do you get angry or frustrated? Do you lash out? Does your blood pressure go up?

Think about your average day—even yesterday. What did you get mad about that, when you think about it, really didn't matter in the long run? Someone didn't hold the door open for you, and you assumed that they would, and you didn't grab it in time, and it nearly smashed you in the head. You probably got mad; maybe you even said something to that person. Your blood pressure went up, and you went back to the office and maybe told a couple of people. You couldn't believe how rude that person was.

Now what happens? Usually, a cascade of misfortune follows. The coffee maker broke while you were gone. The photocopier ate your original document. Life is just happening, but how are you doing? Like so many people, you're just getting more furious as the day goes on.

This is the majority of stuff that doesn't matter. Things that occur daily that in one, or two, or five years from now won't change the course of your life. It's not the event that's created your anger or frustration—it's the THOUGHT of how you feel about the event.

So now we're back to the mind/ego. What if we could just simply get rid of that thought. How would you feel?

Probably great, because without that thought of the event, there would be nothing to get angry about. Pretty cool, right? But it's easier said than done.

This is where soul setting comes into play. Is the outside world corresponding with your inside world? Probably not. "This isn't supposed to be happening to me, why does this always happen to me." Negative emotions thrive on negative experiences and thoughts. The ego loves to be right, and it will give you more reasons to prove that it's right by showing up in different ways to create issues with your life. One thing after another seems to go wrong.

When things go wrong, it's an opportunity for you to grow. What do I mean by "grow"? Your inner peace and freedom are subject to various situations and circumstances (not problems), and they let you know where you need to grow. Perhaps you need to grow in patience and relaxation. One of the purposes you're here on Earth is to grow spiritually, to have a world of inner peace so most of the mundane occurrences that happen in daily life don't bother you as much.

What to Do and How to Get There

First, breathe. Then ask yourself these important questions: Is my inside world matching my outside world?" Most of the time, the answer will be, "no." Will this issue affect the next one, two, five years of your life? Will it alter your life's direction? Again, the answer usually is, "no." Then, let it go.

Easier said than done. This is why it's so difficult in the beginning. Your mind has created a path of resistance to the circumstances of daily life. When things in the outside world are not the way you think they should be, you tend to go back to your identity, which, for a lot of people, is anger and frustration.

And by the way, when it comes to doing this, I'm guilty, guilty, guilty. If I'm to be totally honest in this book, I must admit that this is one of the struggles I deal with. In my early twenties and thirties, I would throw things and have tantrums. But in coming to this realization in my late forties and early fifties, my life has become different. Is it perfect? Of course not. It's challenging on a daily basis, and sometimes I revert back to my old identity. But this is what we're trying to do here. We're changing our identities. We're trying to change the way we behave in different circumstances and situations.

Every day, stress kills. No, it's not one particular event that kills you, but the accumulation of events over the years. It takes its toll.

The Relationship Between Patience, Time, and Energy

For success to occur in your soul, you must understand that time is an illusion. It really doesn't exist. Yes, we use it to accurately tell someone to meet you somewhere, and we use it to refer to someone's age, but if you consider it, time is the same twenty-four hours day in and day out. You can't stop it or control it. Time will go by whether you are standing still or moving.

Yet, time is the one commodity that's precious because we

all have one thing in common where time is concerned: no one is sure how much of it we have. Some have minutes and some have years, but at some point, each human will run out of time before he or she is called home.

I really believe that everything happens, not for a reason, it just happens. EVERYTHING. Many people think "Why did this happen?" and they continue to look for a reason when in fact there isn't one. IT JUST IS. In my case, as I mentioned earlier, my higher power is God, and he has divine power and control of the world and sets in motion some events that are traumatic (if you let them be), and other events that are utter, complete joy. Knowing that these conditions can happen at any moment, you can put your full energy into the NOW. Don't worry about the past or the future because you can't control either of these things.

Patience is the key to understanding that whatever is to come your way will do so when you're ready, both internally and spiritually. Remember, we all have the same purpose, to help one another and to grow spiritually. Without learning and growing, most of us will go to our graves not understanding soul setting, or developing a soul that is at peace with the outer world because it matches that outer world.

We live in an instant gratification world. If we want something, we can order it off the Internet, and in a matter of days (or sometimes hours or even minutes) it arrives at our doorstep. In the case of furniture, vehicles, or any other household item, all you need is to be approved for a loan, and you can make monthly payments for that big-screen TV and enjoy it in your living room fairly instantly. Technology is moving rapidly, and that gratification will be even quicker if we don't take control and learn patience, because it will only create another illusion, like the one we suffer when we don't get that job we think we should get. Remember, everything happens when it's supposed to happen.

Have you ever wanted something only to realize you didn't want it after all? Maybe this has happened to you in the form of buyer's remorse. For example, you wanted that used car so badly that you see the exact make and model everywhere you go (yes, it's an older car, but it's the only one you can afford). Finally, you purchase it, and within two weeks something goes wrong that isn't covered under your used car warranty. It costs $500 to repair. A month goes by, and something else, but this time, it costs $1,000. You start to think, "Man, why me?" Well, why not you? And when the next breakdown occurs, you think, "Why is this happening?"

It might be happening because you wanted the car so badly that you made poor decisions. You got what you wanted, but it took you all this effort and money to realize that maybe it wasn't what you really wanted in the first place.

It's a lesson we all must learn: You don't always get what you want. Your ego will always test you from time to time, but don't fall into that trap. Your ego wants to be right and find things to be right about. But don't fall into that belief system because it will always lie to you. Your soul is what you want to follow, not your ego.

Part of patience is sacrifice. When you constantly give in to immediate gratification, there is no way to obtain true liberation of guilt—as in, remorse over doing something you know you shouldn't have done. It's called "hindsight." It's doing something that your soul is telling you not to do, but your ego pushes you forward, telling you, "yes, yes, yes!"

Learn to sacrifice and listen to your soul. As you develop

in your soul setting, your remorse will lessen, and you won't have those hindsight moments—the moments when you think you should have done something different. Being free from those is a great feeling. It's very liberating, because it means you're doing exactly what your soul says, and your soul never lies. Be attuned to the soul, and the awareness just gets brighter, and your energy level gets stronger. It eventually becomes your new identity.

Generations

Take a look at someone born in the 1930s versus someone born in the 1960s, or even the 1990s. Those eras were vastly different. You had the massive economic depression in the 1930s, where the unemployment rate skyrocketed, and people lost millions in droves. Then, in the 1960s, you had the civil rights movements, and the assassinations of John F. Kennedy and Martin Luther King, Jr. The 1990s brought us from the industrial age to the information age, in which the home computer became common place.

Now imagine growing up in each of these eras. They all had different values, morals, and beliefs. As people grew up in each era, they brought with them an idea of how life should be, and as a result, parents brought them up with those beliefs. Children always thought their parents didn't know anything, and here we are in the 2020s, and children still don't think their parents know anything. It's a different time, but it brings with it the same purpose that it had in the 1930s: helping one another out.

How can a parent who was born and raised in the 1960s

understand what a person in the 1990s is going through? The age difference is roughly thirty years. Somone who is fifty-six years old right now grew up playing tag outside and riding a toboggan all winter. A person who is twenty-six grew up with a household computer. Communication is so different for the two of them. If the fifty-six-year-old wanted to play with a friend, he would call the friend on a rotary phone, and if the line was busy, he would have to get on his bike and ride over to the friend's house just to find out if he was out playing somewhere. Today, if you wanted to meet a friend, you would text him, and the friend would receive the message instantly.

Notice that word creeps up again and again in today's era: "instantly." This is what the 1990s has delivered to us, and so, understanding that patience is at an all-time low, this can give the fifty-six-year-old an understanding of the twenty-six-year-old, who may be generally impatient with a life that isn't happening as quickly as that person might prefer. The fifty-six-year-old's patience is a different kind of animal; he seldom saw "instant" happen in quite the same way.

This example can give you insight into how people's environment, the way they were raised, their values, morals, and beliefs come into play. When dealing with people older than you, you need to realize that they were raised under different conditions than you. In the 1960s, the mother usually stayed at home and the father worked. By the 1990s, in many households, both parents were working to raise a family. The mother wasn't there when the children came home from school every day, which made a huge difference in the environment that children are developed in today.

Let's briefly look at each generation and what made them unique:

The Lost Generation:	Born 1833-1900
The Greatest Generation:	Born 1901-1924
The Silent Generation:	Born 1925-1945
The Baby Boomer Generation:	Born 1946-1964
Generation X:	Born 1965-1980
Generation Y:	Born 1981-1996
Generation Z:	Born 1997-2012
Generation Alpha:	Born 2013-2025

Any given person's grandparent was born in a completely different environment from their grandchild. Therefore, it's safe to say that the values between grandparents and grandchildren will be different as well.

THE LOST GENERATION

The Lost Generation is best known as being the group that fought in World War I. More than 70 million people were mobilized during WWI; approximately 8.5 million of them were killed and another 21 million were wounded in the conflict. Other major events that occurred during this generation were the introduction of the automobile and the proliferation of electricity in the home.

THE GREATEST GENERATION

The Greatest Generation is a term used to describe those Americans who grew up during the Great Depression and fought during World War II.

THE SILENT GENERATION

There are several theories as to where the label "Silent Generation" originated. The children who grew up during this time worked hard and kept quiet. It was commonly understood during their time that children should be seen and not heard.

THE BABY BOOMER GENERATION

The term "Baby Boomer" is derived from the booms in births that took place after the return of soldiers from WWII. Major events that influenced this generation were the Cold War Era, the introduction of the television, and the civil rights and anti-war movements.

GENERATION X

The "X" was attached to this generation with the idea that the generation resisted being defined, with reference to the variable "X" rather than some other characteristic. Major events that occurred and crossed over into Generation Y included the spread of mass media and computers.

GENERATION Y

Also known as "Millennials," Generation Y is the first generation to grow up with the Internet, cell phones, and digital communication.

GENERATION Z

Generation Z characteristics are interesting and specific. Generation Z features avid gamers and music-goers, and they are known for constantly being on the Internet, social media, and mobile systems.

GENERATION ALPHA

Generation Alpha will be the most educated generation but will redefine what a "real education" resembles. They will prioritize skills over degrees, real-world experience, and on-the job training classes. They will expect highly personalized and engaging training.

Health Improvements

In my view, stress creates more physical ailments than just about any other single component. When you look at certain cancers, heart issues, sleep issues, and a whole host of immune system deficiencies, stress alone is a major factor in these health issues. When you're seventy, eighty, or ninety-plus years old, do you not want a quality of life in which you're not bed-ridden, or dependent on some kind of walking aid? Here's your chance to change your future. Of course, I can't predict or guarantee that you won't have certain health issues. But look around at people in their sixties (or older) who have debilitating health issues and think about how their qualities of life might be different if they had lived stress-free lives. And people often tell me that you can't lead a stress-free life. Of course you can't. But if you could eliminate, say, ninety percent of the stress you have, it could facilitate great changes. And most of the issues, circumstances, and situations that occur in your life are drama that you can do without.

Many of your psychological issues may be directly related to your physiological problems—meaning that you could ease your ailments with the direction of your soul. Addiction comes to mind, for one. It's a vicious circle that will affect you from a physical issue. Find a solution for your psychological issue, and your health will improve dramatically. For many, soul setting can be that solution.

> **Growth and change are two different things. Growth is inward; change is outward.**
>
> / Levy /

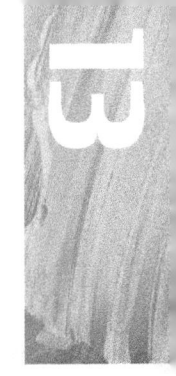

Zen

What is Zen? Zen is a term that describes a feeling of inner peace, oneness, and enlightenment, which means being aware of your inside world. This is achieved not through the mind, but the soul. And don't worry, I'm not going to take you down a path of three-hour meditation sessions and massive amounts of yoga. I don't object to meditation, because to me, meditation is relaxing and breathing. I don't sit with my legs crossed on a mat, either. My mediation is walking very early in the morning for seven kilometers, which takes me about an hour and fifteen minutes. When I walk (including my winter walks), I go out very early because where I live, there's no traffic early. I think about my inside world and look at the outside world and become okay with how things are going. If my results don't support my direction, it gives me an excellent opportunity to create. I love to create. I truly believe that everyone on Earth is bound for creative expression of some kind.

Our anxiety does not come from thinking about the future, but from wanting to control it.

/ Kahlil Gibran /

Traditional Zen is to think about nothing. Finding a relaxed state of oneness. For me, my creation is my nothingness. I love to create, and it's very stress-free. When I compare my outside world to my inside world, there really isn't any friction between the two. I release the outside world and I let it go because I can't control it. And it's not just on my walk that I do this, because my outside world tests me every day on an hourly basis. People say things and people do things that irritate me, but by releasing it and having an awareness of these things, it becomes my new identity. We want inner peace—soul setting is the place for this to happen, and it takes time and practice. Remember, my higher power didn't say to me the day I was born, "Good luck, this world isn't the best, and you'll struggle forever." This brings us to Yin and Yang.

What Is Yin and Yang?

I believe Google has a great definition for yin and yang: "Yin and yang is a Chinese philosophical concept that describes how obviously opposite or contrary forces may actually be complementary, interconnected, and interdependent in the natural world, and how they may give rise to each other as they interrelate to one another."

This is a good way to understand the energy that surrounds us. How do I know there is this energy? Faith. I have a belief that positive things have to happen, and unfortunately, without being delusional, negative things will happen also. When you understand yin and yang, you will recognize that it's a powerful force of polar opposites that you'll learn to appreciate.

For example: How do we know we're happy? Well, we have sadness to refer to. If we didn't have the opposite, it would be impossible to accept happiness or sadness. It's necessary, and it's in all things in this world where opposite energies or forces occur.

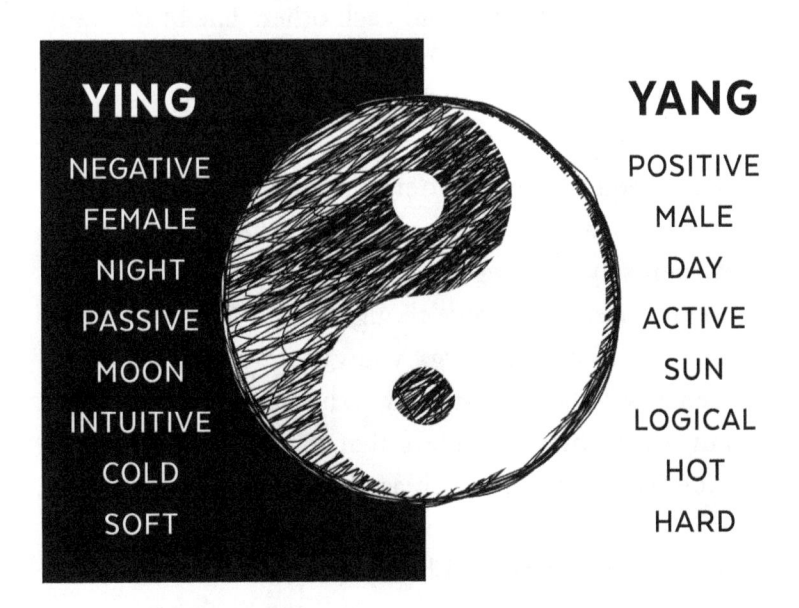

YING	YANG
NEGATIVE	POSITIVE
FEMALE	MALE
NIGHT	DAY
PASSIVE	ACTIVE
MOON	SUN
INTUITIVE	LOGICAL
COLD	HOT
SOFT	HARD

Chi, Energy, and Vibration

Another very important part of soul setting is understanding that we all carry energy and attract energy for our outside selves. This energy can be positive or negative. Chi is your life force, the energy that flows through you and through everything.

Do you know someone who always seems to have bad luck? They are negative to the world and negative to others. The pessimistic attitude they carry is energy that they're releasing into the world. This can be "thought" as well. Where your thoughts go, so does your energy . . . to a point.

Where do thoughts come from? This is a tough question, as it seems that thoughts simply appear from nowhere. My explanation of this phenomenon is as follows: The soul and the mind are independent from each other. The brain is full of neurons that allow us to think, communicate, and move. Thoughts don't come from the brain, they come from the soul. The energy that's around us creates thought, and it's only then, when we give it attention, that the power of the thought has meaning. These thoughts trigger emotion to present themselves in certain ways. Therefore, you should give active awareness to these thoughts.

Understand that the energy you give these thoughts will project energy outside your body. When a negative thought comes into your brain, I believe that that thought is caused by outside factors, factors such as illness, life events, personality difficulties, and substance abuse, all of which can lead to depression and anxiety. When you notice that a negative thought appears, you should give it little attention so that it doesn't release negative energy. The only attention you should give it is the awareness that it exists, and that you must release it and consciously change that negative thought.

But how do you do that?

Don't dismiss it—recognize it as a negative thought. It won't go away, and it will pop up again from time to time. Understand that it's a lie, and that it comes from the mind/ego and not the soul.

Be intentional. Why are you getting this negative thought? Are you tired? Depressed? Full of anxiety?

Breathe. Be aware of your breathing.

Spend time with positive people.

Be grateful and have gratitude (there's that word again!).

Practice, practice, practice. The more you do the things on this list, the more your programming will change. You'll create a new identity for yourself, and the negative thoughts won't appear as often.

Stop giving away your thoughts and your energy. Dwelling on negative thoughts disables your true potential by giving you less energy. You can take someone else's power from them by being negative, but guess what? Whatever power you take from them is also power you take from yourself. The energy of revenge is cruel to the person trying to rob someone else of power or energy. When you think with your mind/ego, you're thinking alone.

Another danger of negative energy is this: If you compare yourself to someone else, you've decreased your own energy, and given it to that other person. You'll try to instill their values in yourself to mimic them, and that's impossible. You're now trying to live up to THEIR highest potential, and not your own. Think through your soul and your creator and have faith in what's going on—that it will serve you to the highest degree, not against you and not for anyone else but you.

STORY TIME

We must lean into the positive energy in our souls. The more you're aware of your negative emotions, change can occur quickly. You become a new person, and your identity changes.

One day while working at a job site, I noticed a client drywalled over a receptacle I had to find. So, I cut a two-inch diameter hole . . . in the wrong spot. I cursed out loud, but quickly caught myself, and asked myself, "Why did I get mad?" Most of the time, it happens because our inside world doesn't match the outside world. I should have known better and not made the mistake I did, but I wasn't paying attention. I had a choice: I could resist it and continue to struggle, or I could accept it and not struggle. I chose to accept it, and by doing so, I took a second to calm down, breathe, and went on to fix the two-inch hole that I made in the wrong spot.

Now let's look at it as if I resisted the outcome. By being constantly upset, my energy is negative. Guess what happens? More things go wrong. I don't have to convince you, because I know you've had this happen yourself. Once I caught myself, stopped, took a breath, and changed perspective, I calmed down. My energy in my soul moved to a good spot, not just in my mind/ego. This is how you know it's in your soul.

Freedom is not given; it can only be brought about by work—work in the soul, not in the mind.

/ Levy /

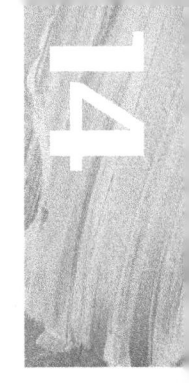

Money

This book is intended for you to achieve YOUR true potential, nobody else's. Within this book the term "success" pops up many times. Just as with the term "your true potential," the term "success" means different things for different people.

One of the most common themes that seems to be appearing is financial stability and living on your own terms. This section will be dedicated to success for financial stability. The definition of "financial stability" means that when a financial issue comes up in one's life, it can be handled with little, if any, repercussion to the balance of your portfolio. In other words, if you had, say, a $5,000 invoice for a car repair, you could handle it without seeing much of a dent in your net worth. You're able to pay for expenditures as they come up with ease.

If you're going to be financially stable, I suggest you start early in life. It's much easier to sacrifice early when you're

---

A big part of financial freedom is having your heart and mind free from worry about the what-ifs of life.

/ Suze Orman /

younger, and your habits regarding money will dictate your future. If you're a spendthrift and purchasing stuff on a whim, then your sacrifice just isn't there. I have an expression that I've taught my children: "Pay now and play later or play now and pay later." What that expression means is that you have to pay your dues and sacrifice at some age. If you choose wisely, you'll sacrifice material possessions at an early age when you can invest your money, and it will compound over time. If you choose to invest at an early age, you'll appreciate it in your mid-forties and fifties, and play can then go on at that time. If you choose to play at a young age, your ability to pay later (meaning investing) becomes more and more difficult, as time is now not on your side. Frankly, this is the case for most people. They play early, and then the catch-up begins.

If you have a side hustle that you want to make into a career (and your main source of income) because you absolutely love it and it helps other people with their lives, never think of the money as the main reason why you're doing the side hustle if you want to make that transition. The transition is difficult to make. In most cases, the money will not be there because your energy is negative. Never EVER think about the money; think of the customer first. If you concentrate on the customer and on becoming the best in your field, the money will follow. The market will always tell you how good you are. Money is just a by-product of what you do and how well you do it.

When you're starting out on your new journey, if you find yourself caught in a place where you're just not able to get to the next level, take a look at what I call your patience and time indicators. Are you impatient? Do you want things

RIGHT NOW? This is a great indicator that you're living from a mindset and not a soul set point of view. Remember that you need to live from an outside world view. You are exactly where you are supposed to be, and resisting this internally just leads to struggle. Let life happen on its terms. You, in the meantime, must always think long term.

What is long term? Ten to fifteen years out, and if you're much younger, you can think longer than that. And here's the real kicker: The fruits of what you do today may not appear for three to five years. Business results seem to take that long before you wind up in a great spot.

If you say to yourself, "I can't wait to work for myself because I'll have more free time, then my suggestion is that you avoid becoming self-employed at all costs. If you want to be successful, your hours are going to be longer. Accept that fact. I believe that most people considering self-employment should not even look at it. IT'S NOT EASY. Yes, there are people who claim in the next three months that, "You, too, can be making six-to-seven-digit figures!" Remember, if it sounds too good to be true, it usually is. Move on, and don't fall victim to FOMO (Fear of Missing Out).

Financial Intelligence

Contrary to what others say, however, you require money to maintain a proper life. Financial issues are often a major reason that couples end married life. This should tell you something about who you will date. Make sure you date someone who is on the same page as you when it comes to spending, saving, and investing. At some point, I'll write a book about financial literacy, and believe it or not, it's not that complicated.

I'm not a fan of endorsing any old book; it really needs to speak to me before I mention it. For now (until my financial book comes out), I encourage you to read Robert Kiyosaki's book, *Rich Dad, Poor Dad*. In his book, Kiyosaki' lists some basic principles you should follow. They are:

> Most people work for money—rich people have money work for them.
>
> It's not how much money you make that matters— it's how much money you keep.
>
> Rich people acquire assets—not liabilities they think are assets.
>
> Invest in YOU.
>
> Live below your means.
>
> The more you give, the more you receive.

MOST PEOPLE WORK FOR MONEY—RICH PEOPLE HAVE MONEY WORK FOR THEM.

The average person works from nine to five (or thereabouts), and either is on salary or punches a timeclock. If you don't work, you don't get paid, period. Rich people put their money to work for them. While they sleep, their money is working. Some examples are purchasing real estate, dividend yielding stocks, putting money in a business as a silent partner, or putting money into a retirement plan. These methods do not produce money from your time; they produce money over time. Each of these examples are different in that the growth of the product may be in the form of interest, dividend, or cash flow that you never touch, and you automatically reinvest.

IT'S NOT HOW MUCH MONEY YOU MAKE THAT MATTERS—IT'S HOW MUCH MONEY YOU KEEP.

I've known people who make $250,000 a year, and they're broke. Why are they broke? Because they feel they have something to prove to the world. They go out and lease a huge BMW, their mortgage payment on a million-dollar house is outrageous, their vacations cost a mint, and their lifestyle is impossible to maintain. I have also known people who work in a factory making $50,000 a year, and they're millionaires. How? They invest in assets that produce income as well as appreciate, meaning that the product they purchase goes up in value over time. An example of a product that *doesn't* go up in value over time is a vehicle (with the exception of exotic or antique vehicles). We are talking about everyday vehicles that people use on a daily basis.

RICH PEOPLE ACQUIRE ASSETS—NOT LIABILITIES THEY THINK ARE ASSETS

What are assets and what are liabilities? According to Kiyosaki, assets put money in your pockets, while liabilities take money from your pockets. In his book, he mentions that cash flow is the key. And based on these definitions, something is only considered an asset if it provides you with positive cash flow and puts money in your pocket.

Here are some examples of assets:

> Real estate/rental properties
> Businesses
> Mutual funds

Here are some assets of liabilities:

> A home (mortgages, taxes, repairs)
> Car/boat/plane
> Club memberships
> TVs/clothes/jewelry

Characteristics of a financially literate person:

> Understanding the concept of time
> Sacrifice
> Patience
> Discipline
> Delay gratification
> Invest in self
> Donate to causes
> Faith

A financially literate person MUST master these principles in order to create wealth.

Time is just an illusion. It doesn't really exist; it goes by if you don't pay attention to it. Have you ever been doing something you really enjoy, like going to a party, and you've been there for three hours, and the time flies by? Or have you ever been in a three-hour lecture that you don't enjoy listening to, and the time just drags? It's the same three hours!

There's a saying that the older you get, the faster time goes by, and it's so true. The reason time is an illusion is that the actual flow of time doesn't match our physical reality. We use just our five senses when dealing with time. We have a sixth sense—our soul—which most of us don't tap into, and as a result, we have struggle in our lives.

Sacrifice, in terms of wealth creation, is self-denial and rewarding oneself. It's when you understand that time plays a huge part in your life, and you understand that sometime in the future you will be rewarded.

Patience is the ability to accept and tolerate delay without getting upset or angry. Out of the seven factors listed here, patience is the soul. If you understand time, then patience will follow. These two factors tend to go hand in hand. Without understanding one or the other, you will have a difficult time allowing yourself to grow your wealth.

Discipline is a key component to wealth. It's a critical factor, and you should schedule a routine of habits to set aside a percentage of your income to invest so that time can take care of accumulation.

Delaying gratification is where many, many people seem to go wrong with wealth creation. It's the old "Keeping up with the Joneses" syndrome, and people just want "stuff." This stuff will have a negative effect on how fast and how much money you will have in the future. When you want something like a TV, a car, jewelry, clothes, and other things that will go down in value over time (or in other words, depreciate), it is an endless supply of stuff. This stuff does impress people to a certain degree, but if that's what you're after—impressing people—then good luck. The "fake it 'til you make it" plan will not work. Learn to delay your purchases until one of your assets can purchase it.

Investing in yourself has to be the toughest lesson to master. This takes time to see the results (just as is the case with anything we want). We want to tangibly see results in our lives to believe such actions will end in the result we desire. I've invested thousands and thousands of dollars into myself to become who I am fifty years later. I do wish I'd done this years ago, but like I always say, at least I didn't wait to do this until I was in my eighties.

STORY TIME

If you're like me, you've already heard of the principle, "Invest in yourself." This means you need to spend money to learn. Simple enough. It's not like I didn't hear this principle when I was younger, but to actually spend money on something that I may or may not get results out of just wasn't in my belief system. When I wanted to start a Shopify store or an Amazon store online, I didn't even know where to begin, so

I started investigating whom to look at and what programs to invest in. I found a company, and in the beginning, it was free—just enough to look easy and to obtain a boatload of money. Then, I needed $1,500 for the first course, so I borrowed it and paid. My only reason for doing this was strictly for the money—I really needed it. So off I went.

    I enjoyed the course, and so I bought the next one, and the next one, and as I went forward, the courses were getting more and more expensive, until I got to the point of spending around $7,000. Naturally, as in anything where you're just chasing the money, it failed, because I really wasn't into it. As time went on, I found more money, and decided to write my first e-book. Not knowing how to get it out there with a sales funnel (which I had forgotten how to build), I hired someone to create one and capture email addresses. When he finished, I tested it, and in the beginning, it welcomed people to my book. I asked the guy who created my funnel to make it more personable by adding the potential customer's name ("Hi, Levy" or "Hi, Sam," for instance), and the guy said it couldn't be done. If it weren't for me taking the course, I would have just said, "Oh, okay." But I explained to him how it could be done. Saving myself thousands of dollars, I fired that person, because he turned out to be incompetent. Taking the course taught me a great deal, and I never regretted taking it, as it has propelled me to take more courses.

Donating to causes isn't discussed in the realm of wealth accumulation as much as it should be. Remember that your two purposes in life are to grow spiritually and to help one another. It doesn't matter if you're not wealthy—everyone should give what they can financially. There is a universal law that states, when a favor is done for someone, then you will be helped in return. I'm a huge believer that God, the universe, or your higher power will follow this rule. It's called the law of reciprocity.

Caveat: a warning! When you donate financially to a cause that's important to you, that's where it ends. YOU ARE TO GIVE WITHOUT EXPECTATIONS. I've seen so many people take what I've said, "give money because Levy said there's a law of reciprocity so I should get something back," and they don't. This is where soul setting comes into play. Here, you're giving with your ego/mind with the expectation of getting something back. When you give wholly and freely, you put that feeling of joy into your soul and walk away. Whatever happens after that just happens. If nothing else happens, that's okay. You've given because that is part of your purpose in life, and because you were blessed with wealth. The inner feeling that is created is joy.

Oprah once said in an interview, "I give because I have. This, fundamentally, is where people go wrong. Oprah gives $10 million to a charity, and that's beautiful, and we look at that and say, "Someday, I would love to give that amount." That's where the issue is. We're looking at the amount of money.

EXAMPLE: Oprah's net worth is approximately

$2.6 billion. If we look at the percentage of what she gives versus what she owns, it's about 2.6 percent. Now, let's look at your net worth, and for the sake of discussion, say that it's one million dollars. You decide to give $35,000 to a charity. This $35,000 looks small compared to the $10 million Oprah gave, but in comparison, you really gave more from a percentage point of view.

Now, I know what you're saying: What average person has a million dollars, and $35,000 to donate to charity? This, however, was an experiment to show that if you look at the data in a different way, it will create a different perspective.

I truly believe that donating your wealth is important to financial literacy—that's why this section on this topic is bigger than the others. Why isn't it number one? Well, all the topics are important and work together. Without one, then it will be difficult to accomplish wealth creation.

Faith. My faith is in a higher power that is creating each divine moment. For me, that higher power is God. It's taken me 50 years to realize that God is creating moments for me to learn; God isn't rewarding me or disciplining me for my errors on this Earth.

Soul setting has played a huge part in my wealth creation. Through soul setting, I've had faith that solutions always work out for the best, even if I don't see them at the time, but I've had that faith in my soul, and not my mind/ego. I really believe this to be true. We're all going through this world the best way that we can. Without a lot of optimism and a positive attitude for a future that looks bright despite the traumas and hard times, God is really looking out for my best interests, always. We may not see it at the time, but I can assure you that if my life didn't take quite a few bumps along the way, it would not have brought me to the point of writing this book and helping others.

Soul setting has really helped me in this method of wealth creation. I have been more aware of opportunities. And when hard times come, I realize it's a chance to flex my muscles in the spiritual growth department and learn about what life is teaching me. I don't take tough times with a knee-jerk reaction and say, "What is happening to me?" And yes, I fail from time to time, because I'm human. Always remember that each minute, good or bad, is trying to tell you something about your spiritual inner peace, and it brings you closer to where you'd like to go, and more importantly, where you *need* to go. Wealth is a byproduct of inner peace.

Increased Wealth

You'll notice that I mention this last. Often you might hear, "Money isn't that important," or "There's more to life than money." I really don't believe these things to be true. Here is my truth: Money is important, because without it, how do you pay your bills? How do you eat? How do you pay for shelter? It's just that simple.

I just want to live comfortably. What does that mean? People say it all the time. They usually mean they just want to be able to pay the bills, eat, pay their rent, maybe go on a nice trip once a year. They never mention anything about investing money or donating money. Sure, they say they'd like a little nest egg, but that's where it ends.

When you understand soul setting and what it can do

for you, the opportunities it provides because of the elimination of negative energy is quite exciting. You don't have problems anymore because you understand that this is life, and that problems are just situations and circumstances you have to deal with, and that's it. People don't bother you like they used to because you understand their histories, experiences, upbringing, values, beliefs, and morals. You realize that everyone is different. The career you choose is the career you love, and it's not just a nine-to-five job. No, you don't have to be self-employed or an entrepreneur to enjoy life and the abundance of money that it offers. The materialistic objects that you used to simply purchase to keep up with the Joneses no longer show up as frequently as they once did. You no longer compare yourself to that kind of world. You are doing your own thing. You understand that it's not how much money you make, but what you do with your money. Patience and time are on your side, and you understand about wealth-building through asset producing income versus liabilities that drain your pocket. It's a different life when you think with your soul and not your mind.

STORY TIME

When I was in my late forties, like many other people, I decided to jump into Amazon sales. In short, I would be using the giant online marketplace to sell other people's products. This was to be my golden nugget—it would be how I was going to be wealthy.

It all started with a Facebook ad for online stores.

CHAPTER 14

Intrigued, I watched the accompanying video. This person was going to show me how to create a store, design a sales funnel (what the heck was a sales funnel?), and guide me through a course on how to achieve wealth and success. (Of course, this person never actually *promised* me riches, but his sales pitch demonstrated to me that anyone could be rich.) For the low, low price of $79.99, I could watch the introductory example of how this could all happen.

I pulled out my wife's VISA card and purchased the introductory video. I watched it, and was impressed! I could already see the money rolling in. Watching the introduction, I had no idea how this was all going to work, but I felt confident that I could do it. After the introduction, I purchased the next video for $1,200 . . . and the one after that, and the one after that. I ended up spending a total of $7,000 for the entire course.

There I was: I had built my first sales funnel, had emails ready to go out—I even found a product online to sell that I believed in (I was also paying for services that totaled around $225 per month, too). Keep in mind, this was all borrowed money, so this had to work. I prepared my sales funnel for more than six months, and when it was done, I wasn't really crazy about it, but it was finished. It was a money-making machine ready to be unleashed upon the world. The only problem I had was that I had no one to sell my product to.

It was at that moment, with many months behind me of work, of trying to figure this whole thing out and not really enjoying the entire process . . . that I quit.

That's right, I gave up. I was in tremendous debt, but the relief I felt in my body at the thought of going in another direction (never mind that I had no idea what that direction would be) was overwhelming. Online sales would not be my golden ticket. What an "ah-ha" moment!

Jump ahead a few years. I turned fifty, and I took a good look at my life. I was broke. I owed hundreds of thousands of dollars—not in mortgages, but in personal debt to suppliers, friends, and family. I was scared. I really didn't know what to do except to continue down another path that I had found: real estate. I enjoyed it a lot, but I wasn't making a lot of money. My dream was to build a business from the ground up, but it was too expensive, and I couldn't find an investor to help.

It was then that I made a decision that changed not just my career, but my life.

Advertising and Marketing Plots to Avoid

Let's look at life and how it relates to your purchasing power.

Today's technology shows only the pretty stuff. The zillions of dollars you can make doing the things that so many others are doing. The flashy restaurants, the houses, the bling, the vacations, the lifestyle most people would love to have. Is it realistic for the average Joe? Of course not. Marketing agencies over the years have devised words that entice you to believe that you can obtain instant wealth, and in some cases, wealth beyond your imagination. While I believe there is huge abundance for us all, not very many will get there because of mind setting.

When you see someone living a life you would love to have, it sends messages to your brain like, "You can do that," or "Why aren't you working on that?" While some of you can do that, when you go through your mind, self-doubt creeps in and sabotages your ability to act on your ambitions. If you don't know how to handle $100, how can you expect to handle millions? This is what you're looking at. The end product, versus the actual journey of getting there.

Marketing words like "secret," "amazing," "manifest," "undisclosed until now," and "confidential" are descriptive words that entice you to look further into something. How many of you have heard of this: "Now you can learn the secret to weight loss?" Or "You, too, can become a multi-millionaire within a year." Don't get me wrong, I'm not saying it's impossible. What I'm saying is that it's unlikely you will become a millionaire in a year, or even in your lifetime.

There is an old saying, "If it sounds too good to be true, it must be." Or "Why isn't everyone doing it?" I've lived my first fifty years with the notion that I can do whatever I want. What a crock. You can't do whatever you want and be successful.

This book isn't here to rain on your parade. It is, in my opinion, the greatest chance you will have to succeed, and that is to live your life in reality. When you live in delusion, it's a waste of time. You should be living according to the gifts that you're given at birth. Can you imagine if everyone was a skilled surgeon? That's impossible because there can only be so many skilled surgeons. And what if nobody was a teacher to our children? Or there were no police to protect us? These are just a couple of examples of the types of gifts people have.

Gifts are talents that are given at birth. These talents can range from an actual skill to a specific career. When you hone in on your gift, you can find it by looking into what you find is relatively easy for you and more difficult for others. It comes naturally to you. For example, if you can talk to strangers with ease, this is something you should be aware of. What kind of work involves talking to strangers that will help service this world?

Anyway, let's get back to the topic at hand: marketing terms that will drive you into bankruptcy. Usually when you're in trouble financially, you tend to reach for delusional outcomes. You start to Google things like, "How to get lots of money fast." I don't have to tell you that when you type in this actual phrase, you'll get millions of results that come up. If you can focus on your soul setting and understand where you are right now, you'll see that you're financially in trouble. Period. It's not where you want to be, but you're there. Breathe, and do not resist your situation, or you'll continue to struggle. Accepting that this situation is not permanent will help you get free. Sure, you may lose your car, your house, but honestly, is it the end of the world? It's embarrassing and humiliating, and it may set you back temporarily., but it's not the end of the world.

I personally have lost the house I lived in as well as a rental property; these two properties were my real estate portfolio at the time. The company where I worked closed after sixty years, and I lost my job. My tenant didn't pay rent and my rental had a fire, and I had to pay a $1,000 deductible that

I didn't have. I fought this for six months, and finally I had a white piece of legal paper stuck to my front door telling me that I had been evicted and that the bank was taking over the property. Looking back, I survived, and I'm so much further ahead. I'd finally accepted my situation, and the stress was gone. No more resisting. Often, when we take a hard fall like this and you stay positive and have faith in your future, you bounce back in an even better position than you had been in before.

When you hear those marketing words that seem to lure you into a particular product, I use the old saying we mentioned before: "If it sounds too good to be true, then it probably is." Or "If it's so good, why isn't everyone doing it?" I'm not suggesting that you can't get rich, or you can't lose weight in the time that the ad is suggesting. However, in most cases, you just can't. I immediately take this ad, put it deep in my soul, and move on. I forget about it, and never dwell on the "What ifs" or "I wonders." I've never fallen for these ads again.

Contentment

Are you sick of people saying, "I just want a happy life, and to be happy." That is their life goal. And it's awesome if you can do that. I understand what people want. It's the same thing everyone wants: a life that isn't full of drama and stress. They want that inner peace. They want to stop that chattering in their minds.

Here's the issue, however: You can't have a HAPPY life and be happy. It's impossible. Happiness is an emotion, not a state. What you should be striving for is a content life, one with many happy moments in it. Contentment is so overrated. And I don't mean to say that you should just accept life as it comes, doing nothing all the time. When people hear me say, "Strive for a content life," they sometimes get this message mixed up. You won't get the life you want by sitting on the couch, eating potato chips and drinking a beer, waiting for someone to knock on the door and ask you, "Hey, are you looking for a $100,000 a year salary career?" Life doesn't happen that way. You need to put huge effort into your life if you expect huge things back.

Conclusion on Financial Literacy

Most people will struggle through their lives with very little to show, not understanding this concept. Most people that are motivated will say to themselves, "I will become a millionaire." Sound familiar? Of course, you may be in that state right now. I know I was in my early twenties, my thirties, and my forties. We tend to think in large chunks. "How can I make a million dollars?" This is so wrong on so many levels. How do I know? I lived it for fifty years.

Want to know the right answer? The answer is, "How can I *create* a million dollars?"

This is where points three and four come into play. Patience and discipline. A person making $40,000 or $50,000 a year investing in assets that create wealth over time—that person will win. I've seen it, and before the advent of the

Internet. We live in the greatest abundance of any time in history. The Internet has made more millionaires than any other vehicle, and at a quicker pace. I know, I know, I said "patience," and I still mean it. Get a nine-to-five job and start a side hustle you enjoy doing that will make you money. If you don't know how to do this, then this is where principle number six comes into play. Invest in yourself. I'm serious; spending money on a course that's reliable and that will teach you how to do this will be immeasurable down the road.

> **Your perception is your reality. Until you widen your perspective, you will never change, and you will constantly reinforce your narrow world.**
>
> / Levy /

Conclusion

There are many unique perspectives that perhaps you haven't heard about, and some you may not agree with. That's okay. As you learn more about soul setting and start your new journey towards freedom of the mind, I encourage you to have an open mind about what we've discussed in this book. Remember that your past is just an event that happened; it does not define who you are or who you're going to be. Unfortunately, many people will give up because their mind/ego will continue to run their lives. They will fall back to their old ways, because for them, change is difficult, and they will try to justify their past in their mind—something that is futile and impossible. I've found that it's more exhausting to worry about the past, and I can't change the future because all we have is NOW.

Getting your crap together requires a level of honesty you can't imagine. Ain't nothing easy about realizing that you're the one who's been holding yourself back this whole time ... that your lack of discipline is the answer to some of those "Why me?" questions you're asking yourself ...

/ Unknown /

As you move from thinking with your brain to thinking with your soul, there will be times that you revert to your old ways, because your ego doesn't like this process. The ego will want to convince you that you have enough evidence from your past to prove that you aren't enough, that you're too fat, too dumb, too whatever. Your ego will try to keep you from your true potential. When this occurs, your awareness will now be on guard, and you can now recognize, "There's my mind playing tricks on me and lying again."

Remember, your life is one hundred percent your responsibility, and not the responsibility of others . . .

. . . IT JUST IS!

With Deepest Compassion and Love,

Levy

Acknowledgements

I'd like to thank the friends, family, and acquaintances who have hurt me over the years. I've been so blessed to figure out why this has occurred to me so often. It never happened *to* me, it happened *for* me.

Going through life as a victim can be so defeating. Struggle after struggle can be exhausting. Let's face it, people can look at their lives at different stages and say to themselves, "What's the point?" I have had very few friends, and I mean actual friends, upon whom I can rely, and that's okay. I've been blessed with others who have entered my life, like Laurie Brescacsin, Brian Mansell, and Steve Brown, who, in my toughest days, encouraged me to follow my faith and count on God to work this out instead of me. And that definitely turned out to be the case.

Although some family members are still estranged, I feel in time, they'll improve. For now, I have to accept that this is the way things are as of the writing of this book.

We are doing the best we can with what we know.

The defeating moments, the days of massive depression/anxiety, medications, addiction to alcohol, suicide planning, and the many hours of crying by myself in the basement struggling minute by minute to get by seem like yesterday. Those days no longer exist, nor will they ever appear again. How do I know this? I've had some pretty brutal things happen in the past two years, things that would have devastated me years ago, but the dark thoughts never even crossed my mind. I never thought of drinking, or taking my own life, or being depressed or full of anxiety.

Soul setting is definitely the way to go for anyone who is struggling, or for anyone who has had pain in their past that they have to get by. My life is now filled with purpose, pleasure with new relationships, health benefits, and huge financial gain.

I would like to thank my brothers and sisters who at times drive me nuts, but I'm sure I drive them nuts as well. From as early on as I can remember, being the youngest of five with a twin sister, you have all pushed me to obtain my own identity. Thank you.

My parents (George and Ruby, aka Dad and Mom) have always supported me with unconditional love through my tough times and my growth times. They've helped me financially when needed, they've given me a shoulder to cry on when necessary, and most of all, given me the character traits that I've developed because of them: a great work ethic, compassion, caring, resilience, generosity, honesty, and integrity. These are morals and values that I've tried to pass on to my own children. No amount of gratitude could ever repay you. I love you.

There is also a lady who has been in my life; all my life including birth, who has supported me in time of financial woes, in my failures without judgement, and continues to lend an ear for guidance, and has been like a second mother to me. It is totally impossible to ever show you how appreciative I am. Love you, Aunt Shirley.

Lastly, for more than twenty years, this woman has constantly been by my side. She never ran when I got into trouble. She supported me and never doubted me or my capabilities. She has taught me so much about being myself through her own individual craziness. I love that about her. She has always been supportive with whatever I do, and never persuaded me to do something else when I failed. Love you, HBB.

Finally, I would like to end by thanking God, who has shown me the way to this easy life. He showed me that if you follow your soul and have faith, He is in charge; I am not. He has given me the guidance to accept life on His terms and not mine, especially during the times I didn't see what was right in front of me. Through his support, he gracefully inspired me, and I understand how without him, I wouldn't accomplish anything of this magnitude.

LEVY is a father, husband, grandfather, entrepreneur, and real estate developer in Ontario. For the last 15 years he has lived free of the demons that were ruining his life—depression, anxiety, addiction, and suicidal thoughts. *Soul Setting* is his first book.

Photo: HBB Photography